TURN-AROUND

TURN-AROUND

The No-Nonsense Guide to Corporate Renewal

Marvin A. Davis

CB
CONTEMPORARY
BOOKS
CHICAGO · NEW YORK

Library of Congress Cataloging-in-Publication Data

Davis, Marvin A.
  Turnaround: the no-nonsense guide to corporate renewal.

  1. Organizational change. 2. Organizational effectiveness.
3. Corporate profits. I. Title.
HD58.8.D38   1987   658.4'06   86-29285
ISBN 0-8092-4780-1
ISBN 0-8092-4578-7 (pbk.)

Copyright © 1987 by Marvin A. Davis
All rights reserved
Published by Contemporary Books, Inc.
180 North Michigan Avenue, Chicago, Illinois 60601
Manufactured in the United States of America
Library of Congress Catalog Card Number: 86-29285
International Standard Book Number: 0-8092-4780-1 (cloth)
                                    0-8092-4578-7 (paper)

Published simultaneously in Canada by Beaverbooks, Ltd.
195 Allstate Parkway, Valleywood Business Park
Markham, Ontario L3R 4T8 Canada

To my wife Trudy, daughter Julie, and son Jeff,
whose lives have ended up being a lot
more exciting than any of us imagined

CONTENTS

	INTRODUCTION: YOU DON'T HAVE TO BE SICK TO GET BETTER	1
1	"OH, BOY, WHAT HAVE I GOTTEN MYSELF INTO?"	7
2	TAKING FINANCIAL CONTROL, OR THE S.O.B. IN THE FRONT OFFICE	29
3	FINANCIAL ANALYSIS: NO-BULL NUMBERS	47
4	ANALYZING THE P&L AND FINDING OUT WHERE IT GOES: SOME PERSONAL EXPERIENCES—ITEM-BY-ITEM ANALYSIS	75
5	PEOPLE: LOVE 'EM OR LEAVE 'EM	83
6	MARKETING, OR WHERE DID THE BUYERS GO?	103
7	SELLING: "SO YOU WANNA BUY A DUCK"	121
8	THE PRODUCT, OR "BUT, BOSS, HOW DID I KNOW IT WOULD COST SO MUCH?"	131
9	THE PLANT: "THE PLACE OUT BACK WHERE ALL THE NOISE COMES FROM"	139
10	RESEARCH AND DEVELOPMENT: "WHY SHOULD *YOU* KNOW WHAT WE'RE DOING?"	163
11	BEYOND THE BASICS: OTHER TIPS FOR TURNAROUNDS AND RENEWALS	173
12	TYING IT ALL TOGETHER	183
	INDEX	189

TURN-AROUND

INTRODUCTION
You Don't Have to Be Sick to Get Better

I'm a corporate doctor; that is, over the last twenty-five years I have helped many sick and ailing companies get well. I have also presided over the final days of a couple of them that had gone too far to save.

In today's corporate environment *every company*, without exception, will go through a corporate illness or a crisis sometime in its life, and the company can either safely weather that illness or succumb to and finally die from it.

Corporate illnesses are like bodily ones. They don't appear suddenly, they don't kill immediately, and they produce lots and lots of symptoms.

But I wrote this book because most companies can

diminish the effect of external events that cause a crisis by applying some preventive medicine to their operations before a crisis strikes. What I am referring to when I talk about crisis is a major change in the environment in which each and every company operates. These changes are viruses that attack the corporate body. They include:

- Changes in technology
- Changes in the economy
- Changes in your specific marketplace
- Changes in competition
- Internal political turmoil
- Changes in your cost structure

Most companies respond to these changes—which appear in the form of symptoms, such as mixed levels of pricing in the marketplace or deteriorating market share—with a typical set of reactions. First, they ignore them as aberrations, then they react with disbelief, and finally they *panic*.

The key to keeping any company well and profitable is the same one we advocate for ourselves—preventive care. That is, we must remain lean and trim.

As I write this, I am on my tenth major crash diet. I am in a panic because I have difficulty making it up a long flight of stairs and my wife has started calling me "Fatso." My problem is that when I am happy I like to eat and eat well—French food, Italian food, Mexican food, good wine. So I get fat, and then I panic and go on a diet. One of these days I'll miss the cycle, and there will be a very fat hospital patient.

The fat/lean cycle also occurs in a corporation. What happens is that when things are good the corporation gets fat and happy. There is a proliferation of corporate perks; staff grows; management becomes extremely lax on controls. In short, we get fat. Then suddenly, or so it seems, the world falls apart, we have a crisis, we panic, and it's time to fire half the staff, to stop all travel, to cancel advertising, and to dive into the foxholes.

The corporation that survives this madness is probably lucky because panic situations rarely lend themselves to rational decision making.

The proper way to operate is to be *lean and trim all the time.*

Just think of the additional profits that you can make if your business is lean and trim at all times. In good times you can garner great rewards, and in bad times you are able to survive the economic ills that plague your industry.

The computer and electronics industries are going through this type of self-reevaluation process right now. Their market has changed because of incursion of foreign competition. Their growth has slowed except in specific product areas.

Some companies have built large staffs and inefficient operations during periods of explosive growth when it didn't matter, and now they are forced to cut back. Just think where some of these companies might be today if they had watched every penny during their high-growth phase.

What I wish to provide in this book is the methodology for generating an annual "renewal" to keep your company at peak performance while maximizing the satisfaction and fun that come from running an operation at this level. It's an exercise program for taking off corporate fat and getting your company or division or operation down to fighting trim.

Don't expect anything fancy. I have found over the years that the simplest ideas are the best ones. What I have compiled here are some commonsense approaches to appraising and correcting the course of your business efforts that are based on the best teacher—actual experience.

I wrote this book because American business is going through a revolution. The recession of 1980 through 1983 taught us that American enterprise can no longer afford to operate with unutilized resources. The competition from the Orient and emerging nations requires that we produce our goods and services at competitive costs. This external pressure will not ease in the future. In fact, it will get worse. Therefore, companies must constantly be applying review procedures to ensure that they are operating at the leanest levels they can.

Your company must do more with less and manage all the elements of your business well. Only you as a manager can do this. This book will provide you with a method of sharpening your control skills to a finely honed edge.

If you have a division that is in trouble, the measures I will offer will assist you in making it profitable quickly. The methods I hope to teach you are applicable not only to manufacturing companies but also to any type of operation—from a laundry to a hotel, from an airline to a hardware store. The only requirements are that you know how to read an income statement and balance sheet and that you not be afraid to ask questions of the people who work for you, your customers, your suppliers, and your competitors. In addition, like anything good, a lot of hard work is involved in the activities I have described to you.

The really nifty thing about what I will describe is that you can see results immediately. My book is designed mainly for turnarounds, and the important factor in a turnaround is to see results fast. The programs I describe yield significant results very rapidly, and I wasn't kidding about "overnight."

In one instance, I moved a company from loss to profit over a period of three days. (I won't mention the one that took three years.)

Just for the fun of it, you might wish to keep track of the incremental profits generated by following some of the suggestions that I will give you.

1
"OH, BOY, WHAT HAVE I GOTTEN MYSELF INTO?"

The title of this chapter reflects the feeling of every manager, no matter how seasoned, when facing a reexamination of his or her basic business, or operation, whether it is a reappraisal of a profitable business or a turnaround of an unprofitable one.

If it is the reappraisal of a profitable business, the managers who run various parts of the business will say, "Hey, we're doing well. What does this guy want from us?" And if you are examining an unprofitable business, the task, besides appearing formidable, may have the charm of cleaning someone's dirty underwear.

The tasks you will face in implementing will range from solving communications problems to handling "dirty" problems. That is, you may face the relatively "simple" job of getting your "team" to pull together in this effort when in a profitable operation there is no obvious reason to expend the effort, or you may have to deal with the other extreme of management inefficiencies, insufficient fiscal control, and serious morale problems that exist in a problem division or sector of your business. You may even have to face problems of fraud or embezzlement in such operations.

Now that I have turned you off and you are about to put this book on the shelf forever, let me tell you that this process, when accomplished properly, can be one of the most stimulating experiences of your business career. It's not better than sex, but it comes darn close. What can be better than having happy employees, happy ownership, happy customers, and a growing, forward-thinking organization?

Shaping up a company is like the oft-quoted eating of an elephant: it is done in small bites and is chewed well before swallowing.

I have attempted in this primer to distill a number of experiences in renewals and turnarounds into a step-by-step procedural manual for examining the key operational areas of a company and making them more efficient. The recommendations I make do not require you to have an MBA from one of the most prestigious schools (often it helps not to have one), nor will I quote heavily from the multitude of other business writers in the field. This is a compendium of the practices I have used and my friends have used in the real world. It is reflective of the scar tissue garnered over years of effort and is similar to the lesson you learned as a child when Mama told you not to touch the stove when it was hot and you did it anyway. In my career I have touched a lot of hot stoves and have learned a great many lessons.

These lessons are the result of a great deal of experimentation in attempting to find the right solution to a knotty problem and making a lot of mistakes.

In the text I shall make several assumptions:

- You know how to read a financial statement—both a balance sheet and a profit-and-loss statement.
- You know some of the basic jargon that is common to the business world.
- You know that the basic objective of this exercise is to increase profit.
- You have read all you can about the basic business in which you are involved.

If you don't have these technical skills, a brief course, such as the American Management Association's "Finance for Non-financial Executives," can bring you up to speed very quickly.

OK, enough introductory items. Let's get going!

STEP 1.
ESTABLISHING OBJECTIVES

In a corporate renewal you may think the objective is rather obvious, that is, to make more "profit." So why the hell is this clown talking about establishing objectives? But even in the best-run companies, the long-term objective of the management must be known, since it dramatically affects the actions you take. Let me give you some examples:

Long-Term Objectives

The intent here is to do those things that will ensure the continued operation and growth of the company. The intent of the ownership and management of the company is to have a long-term investment in the company or division. If there is a turnaround involved, the intent is to correct the problem on a long-term basis and prevent it from ever occurring again. This objective brings with it certain long-term strategies and reinvestment options that ensure long-term growth. Examples are investment in research and development and investment in certain types of staff personnel that will have long-term payoffs that cannot be equated to current sales.

Preparation for Sale

Often consultants are brought into an operation to get a company "dolled up" in preparation for a sale. This is a legitimate endeavor and often results in the eventual retention of the company when it becomes evident that the company can be a viable entity. The efforts in this instance strongly influence overhead and equipment investment criteria, as well as personnel decisions. A decision may be made, for example, to add capital to "spruce up" a particularly undesirable facility.

Short-Term Objectives

When a company or a division is using gallons of red ink, the auditors are snapping at your heels, and the bank is threatening to call in its loans, you are *in extremis*, a quasi-legal term meaning "at the point of death" and used in the Navy to describe an impending disaster, such as a collision. In such circumstances, the primary objective is survival, and the action steps necessary reflect the need to save the company without an overly great concern for long-term considerations. It must be cautioned that, once out of *extremis*, a company must attempt to get back into the long-term view, or operations will continue as a series of crises and the company will never operate in a normal mode.

Of course, there are various gradations between these short- and long-term extremes, but the individual charged with renewal should have a clear understanding of the nature of the final objective. If there is any single cause of disillusionment among management in efforts of this sort, it is an unclear understanding of the initial objectives of the effort.

It is preferable to have these objectives in writing and agreed upon by the board or ownership of a corporation before you embark on a renewal. You should also put the objective in a place where you can read it from time to time, because it's easy to forget what the objective is if you are flushed with success from a small victory or despondent from a setback. I once had an associate who was president of a division of a major baking company. This division was charged with making literally millions of a single creme-filled pastry and distributing it worldwide to equal millions of prepubescent kids all screaming for his gooey product. You may feel that it would be damned impossible to forget your objective under such circumstances, but it happened on occasion, so this individual would repeat his objective aloud every morning while he shaved.

Of course, objectives *can* change. It's just that everybody had better be in agreement when they do change.

STEP 2.
SO YOU WANT TO BE A HERO

In this age of enlightened management, I am about to commit a major no-no. I am about to tell you that a renewal requires a benevolent dictator or leader. It cannot be done by a committee, a group, a study organization, or anything of the like. The authority and responsibility must be with a single designated individual. This individual must have the overall leadership role in the renewal, and he or she becomes the motivating force behind the effort.

It is best if the company or division president who already has the power and authority be the guiding light in a renewal effort; however, anyone who is designated can lead the effort. This individual should be imbued with the power to organize the effort and at least to suggest to the president activities in the following areas:

- Personnel decisions
- Strategy decisions
- Investment decisions
- Policy decisions

Let's explore each one of these areas individually.

Personnel Decisions

In personnel decisions, the activity breaks down into two major areas. In a good organization, one that is doing well, the "Renewal Leader" must have the authority to pull together, across interdisciplinary lines, the people necessary to coordinate the renewal effort, and this effort must occur at the highest level possible.

Let me give you an example of this effort. Say that you have been named the Renewal Leader and you, as part of your effort to examine operations, need to look at a computer operation that may be too large for current or foreseeable future operations of the company. Yet the vice president of finance has been convinced that this computerization is the *only* way to go. I faced a situation similar to this when I suggested that a major project in computerizing a production control and production accounting system be delayed until the underlying manual system, which was a mess, was straightened out. The controller in this instance had been convinced that by computerizing the system all his problems would magically disappear, and he had committed himself to the project. Needless to say, I was called everything from a cretin to antiprogressive.

The person who does the renewal must have the authority to say, "Stop; let's reevaluate" and then be able to sit with the controller or vice president of finance and say, "I want you to succeed. Let's work together to see that you do."

Oh, by the way, on the example I cited I didn't convince them immediately, but $250,000 later and after a mess the likes of which you wouldn't believe, the company followed my suggestion.

It is important that the Renewal Leader be imbued with the authority necessary to accomplish the desired effect. In the instance of a poor or failing division, the Renewal Leader must have the authority to make hire/fire recommendations. Remember, when you've got a sick division, the first people to realize it are the internal managers, and good managers are the first to bail out, mainly because they are the most marketable. This becomes increasingly true as the length of time since the troubles began increases, so that by year two or three, there should be virtually no one left in senior management who is motivated or capable of carrying on. These are harsh words, I know, but it is amazing how true they are. You, the "renewer," must have the freedom to gather around you the best and most capable individuals to do the job at hand. You should be sure that you have the support of your management, whether it be the chairman, the president, or other senior management, prior to embarking on this effort.

Strategy Decisions

In the process of renewal, certain decisions will need to be made regarding basic market strategies and financial strategies. It is very important for these decisions to be able to be implemented without a lengthy series of approvals if the renewal is to occur within a reasonable time frame. There should be a clear understanding that action will be taken rapidly and without a lengthy approval process.

Investment Decisions

The person in charge of a renewal, especially a turnaround, should have some clear-cut limits as to approval of spending limits. This may mean parameters such as fixed investment expenditures up to X dollars or a maximum of Z dollars in aggregate expenditures without prior approval of the board.

I have personally operated with only a capital expenditure limit and an understanding of "normal" operating expenses.

Policy Decisions

Often in a renewal you will find it necessary to implement a new policy or to change an unfair old one—again, limits of authority should be established. You do not want to have to go through some laborious approval process to achieve the implementation of a changed policy.

For example, suppose you wish to institute a no-nepotism rule in your organization or you wish to eliminate a discriminatory policy. Be sure that the mechanism is in place to do this without everybody's voting on it.

Again, remember that if you are coordinating this effort you must know the limits of your authority in advance and adjust your approach accordingly. Remember that the fewer approvals prior to acceptance, the faster you can begin to see results.

STEP 3.
GO FOR THE JUGULAR: PRICING

You may consider it strange that I don't take you into a lengthy problem analysis, a market analysis, and a study and formulation of strategy. However, I said that this book is a high-speed primer, and the quickest action you can take is a price increase. The effect is instantaneous. It will increase profit immediately in a profitable company and stem the magnitude of loss in an unprofitable company if not move the company into the black. If done correctly, a price increase has no influence on sales volume. In some instances it may cause an increase in volume, and in most instances it sends a message to the internal management and the sales force that there is a new force at work within the company.

I am not talking about an indiscriminate increase, but rather a well-thought-out, well-planned, and well-executed increase. Even with these criteria, the action can take place within days of your assumption of your new role.

Approaching Price Increases

Here are some basic rules regarding price increases/pricing structure:

- They should be market-driven.
- They should reflect the company's perceived position in the marketplace by the customer.
- They should *not be based on cost*.
- They should always be based on price/volume consideration, not emotional constraints.

What do all those fancy words mean? First, analyze your pricing position in the market as follows:

First, lay out a comparison of the cost of your products as compared with equivalent products produced by your competitors. This could mean doing anything from comparing milling machines to comparing the price of one-bedroom suites in hotels. Be sure to compare actual prices, as well as list prices. This means that you have to compare the net cost of the product or service to the customer, including all discounts from list, freight, terms of payment, etc. These factors often become more important than the list price.

I know a company, and you most likely do also, that prided itself on maintaining the highest list price and its position as price leader in the industry. However, because of its volume discount structure, its willingness to make a "deal" with anybody, and its laxity with regard to receivables, the true price and hence profit margins, were lower than anyone else's in the industry.

Also, ensure that you get the same kind of information for your competitors, so you know what they are *really* charging. This can be done by discreetly inquiring in the trade or by calling your competitors and posing as a buyer. Your sales personnel are also a great source of information in this area.

Often your list prices can be higher than those of competitors, while your net can be significantly lower.

One company I looked at as an acquisition candidate and a possible turnaround candidate had a very nice profit-and-loss statement. But as I perused it, I noticed that near the bottom of the statement, which showed very nice operating margins, was a "seasonal adjustment" that wiped out any profit and, in fact, put the company into a net loss position.

Being inordinately curious, I asked, "What the hell is this?" It seems that each year the company would produce machines in anticipation of the summer selling season, then inventory them. Then, as the season passed, the company would begin discounting the remaining inventory to move it. By late fall the discounts were up to 50 percent, and by winter the cycle would start all over. A simple pricing analysis showed that its average discount was 25 percent and that there was no way the company could make money unless the pricing policy was changed.

Now list at least three competitors' pricing for similar products that *compete for the same business*. This analysis may appear trivial to you, but you would be amazed at the pricing policies that this smokes out. I was involved with a company that had been raising its prices at a rate of 4 or 5 percent a year across the board for a period of the last seven years while the competition had been pricing its product to meet market demand and its perceived quality and position in the marketplace. As a result, the company whose product was perhaps the most expensive to produce was now charging among the lowest prices in the marketplace.

After obtaining net comparative pricing for your products, you must obtain a subjective analysis of your quality and faults. Let's take the same products we used for the pricing analysis and analyze them. What you do in this instance is to dispassionately compare your competitive advantages and disadvantages for each product that you offer on an item-by-item basis with a similar product offered by your competition. Do this on a spread sheet in written form.

These advantages and disadvantages can be smoked out by discussing them with both your marketing and sales groups and your product development group. It is best to have outside sales personnel provide input for this chart, since they have the greatest interaction with the customer and know what the competition is offering. The mere process of putting something like this together is often an eye-opening experience.

The next thing to do is decide where your company's products stand in the customer's perceived hierarchy of products. For example:

"It's the Cadillac of the industry."
"It's a good middle-of-the-road product."
"It's a good low-priced, price-competitive product."

Armed with these items and knowledge of your ability to be a price leader (Will the others follow if you raise prices beyond those of the current competitors?), you now have the ammunition to raise prices and an idea of the levels to which you should raise them.

There is, incidentally, another approach to pricing that is tricky and involves intimate knowledge of your manufacturing process.

Optimizing the Cost/Volume Curve:
A Dubious Approach

This is a decision to optimize the cost/volume curve.

The theory is as follows: If I can get my volume up high enough, my manufacturing cost and overheads will drop on a per-unit basis, and I will make more profit per unit. Therefore, I should lower my price, so people will buy more from me and I can increase my volume.

This is commonly called "screwing yourself." It is based on these presumptions:

- Your competition sits dumbly by while you play with the market.

- Your assessment of volume increases per unit of price decrease is correct.
- You have accurate knowledge of your manufacturing costs by product.

I have *never* been able to make this strategy work; maybe you can. However, I *have* obtained incremental business on a *contractual basis* with a large, new customer based on pricing. This means that the volume at the new customer is sufficient to help absorb overheads. In *no* case should this strategy be carried out if you analyze the price necessary to do this and you are losing money at the gross margin level after commissions have been *deducted*.

One last area of our discussion approaching price increase is proprietary products.

Pricing of Proprietary Products

Proprietary products are ones in which you have an *exclusive position*. Your position may be exclusive as the result of a patent, because some special technical knowledge is needed to manufacture the product or because the cost of manufacture is such that competition is hesitant to copy the product.

There is *no reason* to make anything but a *very favorable profit* on a proprietary item. Believe it or not, a company I once operated had a device for which it had the sole patent but had been selling the product at a loss for 10 years and was considering dropping the line. *That is just plain stupidity*. We raised the price of the product 200 percent over the next year, and it was the most profitable product in the line until the patents ran out three years later.

The trick in using this type of tactic is to raise the

price high enough to create adequate profits but not so high as to entice immediate competition after the patents run out.

Announcing the Price Increase

You now announce the idea of a price increase to your sales force. You will hear the following objections:

"If we raise prices, we will lose all our customers!"
"Our customers buy on price, not quality."
"Our quality isn't good enough; therefore, we've got to discount our prices."
"We will lose long-term business."
"The competition will kill us."

The sales force will *always* fight an increase because a higher price makes selling the product more difficult. I have never run into a salesperson who has chided me for selling a product for too little. (If you have one, please have him pickled in martinis, and send him to me.)

By the way, a price increase does not have to be overt. It can also consist of elimination of discount structure, reduction in credit terms, modification or establishment of a volume-related pricing structure, etc.

If your rationale for increasing pricing is explained to your sales force and they are given the data you have developed in reaching your decision, they will support you in the decision.

The eventual *decision to raise prices will always devolve to the CEO or division president.*

So now you have taken an important step toward increasing your profit by increasing price. Remember that most companies operate on posttax income of 5 to 7 percent. This means that a price increase of 1 percent yields a net income increase of .5 percent after tax, or 10 percent of the normal profit level. Since most price increases are 5 percent or above, this means that you can increase profit by 50 percent in one fell swoop.

STEP 4.
"HEY MISTER, CAN I BORROW YOUR WATCH?"

Now that you have taken your first step toward increasing profits, it is time to go back and do what the consultants do: they borrow your watch to tell you what time it is.

This section is devoted to analysis of the opportunities and problem areas of a company. The best way to do this analysis is to discuss the problems of the company with key managers so that you can identify some of the key problems as perceived by the people who are in place. It also gives you an opportunity to assess the quality of the interviewees themselves. Hence, you are borrowing their watches to tell them what time it is.

Interviewing Key Managers and Others

You should interview the following people:

- All top management (vice president level)
- Sampling of middle management—usually random choices (definitely the personnel director)
- Sampling of the field sales force—both best performers and worst performers
- Sampling of line foremen and supervisors
- Sampling of work force—random selection

The interview process should be informal in nature and honest in approach. You should interview the individuals in private and indicate that you are soliciting their opinions and feelings because you respect their opinions and feel that they might provide some insights.

Ask each of these individuals:

"What do you perceive the opportunities of the corporation to be?"

"If you were president, what would you do?"

These are simple questions, but it is amazing the insight these individuals can provide if they feel that the responses they give are being treated confidentially. In addition, in healthy environments good managers can always see areas in which the operation can be improved.

People in a problem company are usually frustrated by the company's performance and can often verbalize what they view as problems, even though their solution may be simplistic or they may be unable to implement the solution on their own.

Sure, you're going to get some "sour grapes," which relate directly to interviewees' own personal situations. But for the most part, the interviewees' comments will be extremely constructive.

As you conduct the interviews, take notes. Jot down one-liners such as "suggest reduction in order entry work force" and "need more engineering" during each interview. Fairly quickly, a pattern of perceived problems will emerge. You should begin putting these in a matrix as on the facing page.

An x indicates that a particular suggestion emerged in an interview with a particular individual; the lack of an x means that it was not mentioned. An opportunity area or problem mentioned several times means it's worth looking into.

After your first 25 or 30 interviews, some fairly clear patterns begin to emerge about the nature of the opportunities.

NOTES FROM EMPLOYEE INTERVIEWS

Problem	V.P. Personnel	V.P. Sales	Manager Admin.	Manager Engineering	Manager Production	Foreman	Worker
Reduce Order Entry Work Force		x		x	x		
Need to Increase Sales Force Size		x	x			x	x
Raise Wages	x					x	x

I have indicated that you should talk to people at every level in the organization; this means top to bottom. Often the foreman on the line has better insight into problems than the secure vice president sitting in his office. A phenomenon frequently occurs when a person becomes a vice president. He suddenly thinks that his ideas have become divinely inspired and, as a result, are infallible. This results in what I call the "regal syndrome"; that is, he sits in his office and waits for the masses to come visit him rather than going out and visiting his people. Of course, not even a king adheres to this approach, but corporate vice presidents do.

Interviewing Customers and Competitors

The next step is one that you may feel I am mad to suggest. Nevertheless, I would suggest that you interview some of your major customers and competitors. Your initial feeling about this suggestion probably will be that (1) you don't want to air your dirty linen in front of customers and (2) you don't feel that your competition will tell you anything.

First of all, let's look at your customers. They are most interested in having you succeed because they benefit the most if your product/service improves. The questions to your customers should be directed so that they elicit constructive criticism and, in fact, can generate a closer bond with the user of your product or service. Tell them you are asking these questions because you value their opinions.

Ask your customers the following questions:

"How do you find our product? What criticisms or improvements would you make?"
"How would you improve our service? What would you do to improve our ability to serve you?"

"How do you feel that our value/price relationship compares with that of our competition?"

You would be amazed, but I found from my customers, in one instance, that our product was grossly underpriced for the function it performed. We therefore raised prices 20 percent without any loss in volume as a result of this information. The customer was easily able to pass the increase along to the end user, and everyone was happy.

You should also talk to the competition, as I have mentioned, because the competitors always want to talk about their product and what their competitors are doing wrong.

Usually I have a consultant schedule a meeting with the CEO of the competitive company and indicate that he or she is doing a study of the industry. Then I have the consultant ask three basic questions:

"To what do you attribute your success?"
"Who are your primary competitors?"
"What's wrong with XYZ company [your company]?"

It is positively amazing what comes out in this interview process. First, competitors will often expose their entire basic strategy because they are confident that no one else can do what they are doing. Second, they will often pinpoint your success and errors far better than you can.

I have received some of my best advice from competitors at conventions and in casual conversations. *People like to talk about their businesses.*

Now create another matrix for your customers' and your competitors' inputs. You now have key problems that you have identified from a number of sources.

SOLUTION SHEET

OPPORTUNITY/ PROBLEM	SHORT-TERM SOLUTION	LONG-TERM SOLUTION	ASSIGNED TO	IMPLEMENTATION	DATE
1) Lead times for delivery are too long	1) Run inventory of fast-moving items	1) Examine production process to obtain further turn-around without inventory increase	J. Jones	1) Recommend new stocking levels	6/71
				2) Recommend action plan in production for faster output	7/31
2) We are missing children's market	1) Identify items in current line applicable to this market and develop plan for getting to market with economic production	1) Identify new items we should be developing for market and allocate resources	T. Smith (short-term) B. Brown (long-term)	1) Have key identified economics and draft of marketing plan	5/15
				2) New products to be developed and R&D cost	6/15

"Oh, Boy, What Have I Gotten Myself Into?" 27

What do you do with this information? I use a summary method and a feedback system called the "delphi method"; that is, I summarize the data obtained in writing and feed the data back to the executives who helped create the data in summary form. I then ask for their written comments on the specific problem/opportunity and their proposed solutions/action in one week. After a week, I have a staff meeting, and we rehash the opportunities and action steps and solutions and make key assignments for their resolutions. The format of the "solution sheet" looks like that on page 26.

Everyone walks out of the meeting with an assignment and an implementation date.

You have just welded your corporate team into one goal-oriented organization with a clear indication of what each person is to do.

2
TAKING FINANCIAL CONTROL
or the S.O.B. in the Front Office

In any corporation, no matter how well run, a major problem is usually expenses. Money disappears as rapidly as it is made, and no one seems to know the cause of this inordinate drain in cash. No matter how efficient or inefficient the accounting system, you are always faced with examining a historical record of what happened to cash. There are several ways, however, to take positive control of the cash in a company on a "real time" basis. One of these is to *sign all checks*.

SIGNING ALL CHECKS

You may think me insane for suggesting this, but there is no more rapid way to find the places where cash is going and to familiarize yourself with the company's purchasing patterns and suppliers. You may sign several thousand checks a day, but you will begin to recognize whom the checks are for and will begin asking questions about why certain amounts are being paid.

Let me give you some examples of things I have discovered via this method:

- I found the Purchasing Department ordering a seven-year supply of parts for a product we were planning to phase out of the line within three months.
- I found a foreman who was falsifying overtime reports to improve his and his people's take-home pay.
- I found overtime being spent in nonessential departments when sales were at an all-time low.
- I found preferential treatment being given to a single steel supplier because of the "favors," such as baseball tickets, etc., that he was granting a member of the Purchasing Department.
- I found standard items being purchased on an "emergency" basis at premium prices when inventory records showed that we had ample supplies on hand.
- I found massive nonstandardization of component parts of the same size causing us to buy less than economic quantities of several parts that served exactly the same function.

These are just a few examples of the kind of things that you can detect when signing those checks. Certainly, as your confidence level builds, you can ease off this procedure, but you should certainly do it for a period long enough to detect any inconsistencies in spending procedures. The beautiful thing about signing checks is that the impact and control occurs *now* and you are able to stop the horse before it has departed out the barn door.

INVENTORY CONTROL

The next area of immediate control is inventory. I often refer to inventory as "the graveyard of sunken companies." Once when I was controller of a company, I prided myself on delivery of whatever bottom line the president wanted, no matter what the "real results." The way this is done is by playing with inventory and reserves.

Most companies use inventories as the burial ground for mistakes, inefficiencies, losses, etc., and at year end these mistakes come boiling to the surface and illustrate why you have been so short of cash all year. Even more significant, improper control of inventory can cause tremendous working capital drains that, for a thinly capitalized corporation, can spell the difference between life and death.

The initial step to take is to *personally* take a tour of your inventory. Ask for, in advance, a listing of items in finished goods; approximate day's sales of each item based on *current* levels of sales; a list of each raw material item and approximate day's, month's, or year's supply and value; and a list of values in work-in-process.

Now go on your inspection. Determine if the quantities, on a spot basis, tally with the lists given you. Use the "dust test" to determine if items have really moved; that is, the depth of dust on a given item determines the last time it moved. If there is any dust, it means that the item has been in inventory too long.

From the preceding investigation, you will soon find out that:

- Your finished goods in some areas are disproportionate to sales.

- You have too large an amount of raw materials of certain types.
- Your inventories in work-in-process are overstated.

The reason I am so sure you will find this information is that there is *no* company I have been involved with that does not exhibit one or more of the previously stated characteristics. Here's what you do:

Finished Goods Disproportionate to Sales

Have "specials" on the slow-moving finished goods to get inventory levels down to acceptable levels. You should know what acceptable turns are for your industry, but in no case should turns be less than six per year and, more desirably, twelve per year.

Overabundant Raw Materials

Reduce raw materials to match your production cycles. That is, determine the maximum length of time to obtain raw materials and the maximum manufacturing time through the factory, and this becomes the maximum inventory level of each item. The Japanese work with one shift of inventory because they have trained their suppliers to deliver goods just prior to their use and have qualified suppliers, so they can be assured of the quality of incoming goods with a minimum of inspection. Can you imagine the cash that is freed up by going from one month's raw material inventory to one day's inventory?

There are three ways to reduce raw material inventory:

1. Return product to suppliers. (There is usually a restocking charge for this, but most suppliers will take the product back from a good customer.)
2. Sell to your competitors at a discount. (Most com-

petitors will consider an arrangement of this type for components.)
3. Find other industries in which the components are utilized and sell to them.
4. As a last resort, sell to an excess inventory disposal firm. These companies will usually give 40 cents to 10 cents on a dollar and are the court of last resort.

Overstated Work-in-Process

By this time, you have found that your work-in-process (WIP) inventory does not all exist. This is because WIP, due to its subjective valuation process, allows the greatest latitude for slop.

An overstatement of work-in-process can indicate that:

- People are not correctly reporting their production (output).
- You have unreported waste (material).
- People are incorrectly reporting their labor input as productive time.
- You are being stolen blind.

There are both long-term and short-term solutions to these problems.

"Oops, I didn't report production correctly."

Both the long- and short-term solution to this problem is to establish targeted goals of output for each department. These goals can initially be set in concert with the individuals in that department and should reflect levels of output that are above those currently being achieved. Engineered standards can be introduced at a later time, but goals, contrary to public opinion, can be established without the sophistication of engineered standards.

An incentive program can be put in place for achievement of output at prescribed quality. This does not have to be a monetary incentive. It can be a certificate or an award or a beer party or any other nonmonetary incentive. The output should be traced and reported daily against goals, and this output should be certified by the department foreman or manager. This doesn't apply only to factory output. It can be applied to any activity from sales calls to credit applications in a loan office. You should ensure that the reports reach your desk and that you participate in the analysis of both favorable and unfavorable performance plus award and censure for output. These goals can be modified upward periodically to reflect improved performance but always with the agreement of the workers and their supervisors.

"Who, us? Why, we would never waste anything."

I had a facility reporting to me where the employees were chopping up stainless steel components, rather than admitting an error in fabrication. The loss due to waste was in the hundreds of thousands of dollars annually.

The quick solution is to stop all scrap disposal without prior preparation of a material disposition report (MDR) on the product. In the MDR the reason for the loss or error is given, the description of the item is given, and the MDR group must:

- Suggest a method of preventing the error from happening again.
- Identify a method of recovering the product being potentially scrapped, if possible.
- Identify the method of disposal that yields the highest income to the company.

We all make mistakes, and the important thing is

finding a way to place emphasis on the solution to problems, rather than on placing blame.

Using this problem-solving method, I managed to reduce inventory loss at one location from $500,000 a year to a moderate pickup at year end.

"I'm sure we worked the whole day."

The third area is the improper reporting of labor hours as productive time when indeed personnel are not spending time on productive output. Since labor hours are the items most easily accounted for, the tracking of productivity and waste should virtually eliminate misapplication of labor hours. The only way to ensure application of labor is by having the supervisors sign off on labor input. This area is the easiest to control, since you pay personnel based on labor hours.

The only area that you must scrutinize is overtime. My policy has always been to deny any overtime unless approved in advance and then only with an idea of what objectives are to be accomplished by such overtime. This is usually a formal or informal approval procedure that requires verbal or written authorization. I have used verbal authorization and had the plant managers rerationalize the overtime premium in their monthly statement.

"No one ever steals from the company" and Other Myths

The last area is the touchiest—that is, theft. I have caught thieves disposing of goods and raw materials. If you suspect theft, the *only* way to handle it is to hire a professional investigatory organization to detect and capture the thieves. The secret of doing this is to trust *no one* and to hire the professionals yourself. The reports should come directly to you.

Don't try to solve the problem yourself. You're not equipped for it. In fact, you may be facing a conspiracy of several employees.

The hiring of professionals is costly but usually is more than offset by the loss in merchandise and raw materials.

Once the thieves are discovered, be prepared to prosecute to the fullest extent of the law. In this manner, you are telling the world that you will not tolerate dishonesty in the organization and are giving any other potential wrongdoers the clear signal of your intentions to halt this kind of behavior forever.

In addition to taking this legal action, have a security audit performed that will indicate the holes in your security system that allow theft.

In a company where I worked, there was a mining operation, and the truckers would load their truck with ore, go to an automatic weigh scale, receive a weigh ticket for the load (undated), and then transport the load some thirty miles to a depot. The truckers were paid by the number of loads that they hauled. The miners were paid by the number of loads picked up by the truckers.

It is easy to figure out what happened. Since piles of ore are normally inventoried by utilizing aerial photographs and a complicated estimating system, some time passed before the cheating was discovered—a whole mountain of ore was missing.

It seems that the truckers had been obtaining two extra weigh tickets each day by weighing each load twice. Since there was no date stamp, it was virtually impossible to detect without catching the truckers in the act. We were paying both the miners and the drivers excessive amounts.

We solved the problem by putting in an automated scale that was activated by a credit card identifying the "driver," the date of the weighing, and the time of the weighing. We also hired a detective agency to place an undercover driver's helper in the system to find out who was cheating. (It turns out all the drivers were, and we immediately discharged them and brought charges.)

CATCHING THE EQUINE BEFORE IT LEAVES THE AGRICULTURAL OUTBUILDING—EXPENSE CONTROL

You have solved, at least in the short term, two major problem areas. Now how do you control expenses? You have solved this in part by controlling the expenditure of cash; however, how do you get fast control of expenses "before the fact"? The answer is establishing short-term goals. Presumably you have established a budget for the monthly and weekly expenditures of your operations. If not, *do it now*. Here are some typical examples of expenditures:

Compensation
Benefits
Travel and entertainment
Postage
Advertising
Promotion
Telephone and telegraph
Insurance
Rent
Heat (gas and oil)
Research and development

What I typically ask my managers to do in a tight profit situation is to go to short-interval budgeting; that is, we budget on a weekly basis.

Let's take an example. Say that last week the company sold $200,000 worth of goods at a 25 percent gross margin, or you generated $50,000 in gross profit. That means that last week you generated only $50,000 to support overhead, sales, and all other expenses, as well as profit. Given that your profit goal is 10 percent of gross sales before tax, you now have $50,000−10 percent of $200,000, or *$30,000* to spend on expenses other than those associated with production. You now take this number back to your people and say, "You now have $30,000 to spend as you please *but no more*," and a short-interval budget (SIB) is created.

The SIB creates tremendous pressure to take the following steps:

- Reduce staff.
- Reduce all unnecessary expenses.
- Improve production management.
- Improve sales volume.

Short-interval budgeting also imposes the requirement for a weekly review of expenses as compared with revenue generation. You and your staff will soon know *where every cent goes*. Of course, your initial goal may be SIB to attain break-even performance or SIB to lose a smaller amount of money initially. But SIB is an intense method of bringing the problem home to the staff.

The goals should be documented in writing and reviewed as to performance weekly. This means your controller is going to be very busy tracking expenses.

Your managers should be questioned as to any expenditures above the SIB and the reasons for them. An action plan should be developed at weekly staff meetings to correct SIB deficiencies and each manager should have a clear idea of what he or she has to do to correct the situation by the following week.

I will get into long-term budgeting and specific expense analysis in later chapters.

QUICKIE FINANCIAL STATEMENTS

The last "rapid" control item is the quickie financial statement. I have had many controllers tell me that it is too difficult to generate a weekly financial statement, yet it is very easy to do on an estimated basis as a control device. The problem with monthly financials is that they usually are issued five working days, at best, after the monthly close or seven to eight calendar days after the end of the month. This means that, at best, the data you receive are, on the average, twenty-one days old. This may be fine from an accounting standpoint, but it's lousy from a control standpoint.

The primary purpose of accounting is to provide control tools for management. Its other functions, such as public and tax reporting, are only secondary. Your financial manager will most likely be aghast at this concept, but unless you truly believe this, the accounting function will run you as opposed to vice versa. But I digress. The quickie statement can be comprised as follows and should be generated weekly.

Sales—This is generated and reported to you weekly anyhow.

Standard cost of goods or cost of sales—This is an estimated historical number that is usually calculated as a percentage of sales.

Gross margin—This is sales minus standard cost of goods.

Extraordinary manufacturing costs—This consists of

items such as overtime and scrap and other extraordinary plant operating costs. Overtime and scrap should be reported on a weekly basis anyhow, and your plant manager should be able to provide the extraordinary plant items.

Overabsorption or underabsorption of overheads—Your plant manager will know the break-even production point for overheads in the plant. An estimate of overabsorption or underabsorption can be obtained by comparing a few samples of actual production output to planned production output. Don't get too complicated. Then operating margin is gross margin, less extraordinary operating costs and overhead variance. (Remember, this is an estimate.) The above does not account for labor, inefficiency, or myriad other effects, but it is close enough for control purposes.

Sales expense—Commissions can be estimated as a percentage of sales.

Other expenses—We have your controller tracking weekly expenses now.

You now have the basis for a weekly "flash" profitability report. You are now armed with the information required to attack problems on a weekly basis.

The preceding process can be greatly simplified by running it on a minicomputer outside your normal accounting system, because it is an approximation.

You now say, "So what? Now that I've got all this, what do I do with it?"

Let me give you an example. Suppose expenses look reasonable, but operating margins are low due to excessive underabsorption of overheads. You now have to investigate possible areas of remedy:

- Increase volume to cover overheads.
- Reduce overheads to match sales by (1) reducing

factory supervision or (2) reducing semifixed or variable factory expenses.

Of course, I presume you would have increased volume if you could, so the primary action would be to reduce overhead.

Another example would be insufficient margins at standard cost to support operations. This means that pricing is too low or manufacturing methods are too inefficient. Obviously, pricing is the easiest of these to modify in the short term, and I have already described pricing action that should be taken. Methods of modifying manufacturing efficiency will be discussed later.

EXAMINING THE COMPETITOR— "HOW COME HE CAN MAKE MONEY AND I CAN'T?"

Now that you have the beginnings of a renewal under way, it is time to pause and strategize. There must be one competitor who is recognized as the leader in the industry, the most innovative of competitors, the cleverest, etc. Earlier I told you that there was nothing wrong with studying the competition. Now I wish you to extend that investigation. I want you to study the entire way your primary competitor operates his business. This is done by gathering information. Earlier I asked you to obtain 10Ks and Dunn and Bradstreet Reports on each of your competitors. It is now time to do an intensive study on this one competitor.

Here are several ways of doing this study:

- Gather all articles that can be garnered from trade and newspaper publications.
- Get the competitor's annual report.

- Try to obtain a tour of the competitor's factory.
- Use your sales personnel to find out what they can and gather catalogues.
- Use any employees who used to work for the competitor to provide you with any information that they can.

I am not suggesting any illegal means of gathering information, but I am suggesting that you use every available source of information and that you put this premier competitor under a microscope. Study everything you can about his business. Ask the following questions:

How does he sell?
What kind of pricing does he have?
What quantity of inventory does he have as compared with sales?
What percentage of sales does he spend on research and development, marketing expenses, and promotion?
What does he pay his salespeople?

Complete a dossier on your competitor that is as complete as you can possibly make it. List weaknesses, strengths, and so on.

This information is intended as a guide, not to induce you to copy his every move. Often in analyzing your own business, you need a guidepost, and who else provides a better reference point than your major and best competitor? You will later form an independent operating strategy based on what you have learned from this analysis and an analysis of your own business that hopefully will allow you to do better than the "best" competitor.

Place all this analysis on a summary sheet and keep it handy for the next chapter.

THE COMPUTER—WHY IT WON'T SOLVE ALL YOUR PROBLEMS

With all this analysis going on, the first question that comes up is, "Do I need a computer to do all this manipulation of data?" This is not an easy question to answer. I am introducing it at this point mainly because most troubled companies have a screwed-up accounting system, and it is usually the perception of the management that computerization will solve everything.

This is not so. You must first design the information system, decide what you want, and *then* and *only then* decide on a computer and computer system according to those wants. Companies often end up spending a fortune on a computer system, only to find it doesn't do what they want. I will later more deeply probe computer systems and their usage, but for the time being, you should concentrate on developing the manual system for analysis. If your controller can do it simply on existing computer facilities or on a minicomputer, then let him use the tool with which he is most familiar. But *do not* feel that the computer will solve your problems—only your brain power will.

PAYABLES AND CASH FLOW—"WHO ARE THOSE BOTHERSOME PEOPLE KNOCKING AT MY DOOR?"

Cash flow, as you know, is very dependent on your relationship with your suppliers. Most businesses in trouble begin to stretch their payables performance to their suppliers as a way of offsetting losses. This, of course, leads to poorer and poorer credit and CODs and signals the downward spiral that leads to bankruptcy.

There are other ways to stretch cash in the payables area without destroying your credit or hurting your suppliers. Here are some that I have used:

- Extend payment of bills to the maximum that normal industry practices will allow—normally thirty days but perhaps as much as forty-five days or even sixty days.
- Negotiate extended terms with your suppliers for a commitment for your annual requirements of their product on a sole source basis. Often by making such a commitment you can get sixty- or ninety-day terms.
- Schedule delivery of supplies. In Japan, suppliers to major companies provide components and raw materials on a "just prior to use" basis. Japanese factories have no more than one shift's worth of incoming materials on hand. This saves Japanese manufacturers immense amounts of interest. There are, however, two preconditions to establishing this type of relationship: (1) the supplier must be *very* reliable in his delivery schedule, and (2) you must be able to rely on the quality of the goods introduced by the supplier without preincoming inspection or with spot inspection at best.
- Have the supplier establish his inventory in your factory. That is, your supplier puts his inventory into isolated storage in your facilities, and you pay the supplier as you utilize the material. I have done this with sheet steel suppliers, again using the leverage of buying the annual supply from one source or two sources exclusively.

Taking Financial Control 45

You can get the idea of what I am driving at. By doing a little innovative negotiation in advance with your suppliers, both of goods and services, you can cut back cash outflow considerably.

If you are already in an overextended position in the payables area, the above strategies still work and can be used to reduce the financial pressure. If you are operating well, this technique can give you a new source of cash at zero interest with which you can finance that new marketing campaign, the design of that new product, etc.

3
FINANCIAL ANALYSIS
No-Bull Numbers

PHILOSOPHY—SOME PERSONAL FEELINGS

I have stated that I feel financial statements are intended primarily to control the business, not for corporate reporting or tax purposes. I also feel that this is not inconsistent with the latter goals.

I believe that it is essential to have financial control devices in place. No business of any size has managers who are astute enough to operate without financial controls. The personal computer has placed these financial controls and analyses within the economic reach of any organization. Accurate financial documents and an understanding of the interaction of the various elements of the operational statements are *essential* to the efficient operation of a company.

In view of these conditions, it is also essential that *your chief financial officer understand this philosophy and be prepared to respond to your needs for information.* If you cannot elicit this response, you must obtain personnel who are prepared to help you in the manner you need. The pressure on the chief financial officer will be enormous during a turnaround, and you need someone who can handle it.

With all this in mind, let's go through the key elements of analysis of the statement.

BALANCE SHEET ITEMS

Receivables: Or, "Oh, what fun it is to do business, but I can't get paid."

Every company has downturns, and when business is bad you have a tendency to accept a customer's credit when it is less acceptable than credit you would normally accept. What happens in these instances is that bad debts and past dues go up dramatically, which in turn worsens your cash flow situation and makes you more desperate for more business, which causes you to seek even more marginal customers, which . . .

OK, what do you do?

There is nothing wrong with accepting marginal accounts. However, you should identify them, red-flag them when taking them on, and take some precautionary steps. These steps include:

- Personal guarantees from the owners
- Very stringent follow-up as soon as the credit period is over

Financial Analysis: No-Bull Numbers 49

- Heavy penalties spelled out in advance for delinquent payment
- Perfection of liens on equipment
- Domestic letters of credit

A little preparation can save a lot of heartache in the future.

On current accounts you should have an aging schedule prepared on a monthly basis by customer. Use these agings to go after delinquent customers.

Once a customer is late, you should telephone him to obtain funds and send a letter of notification. In any case, you should resend a statement to the customer every thirty days. If the customer is more than thirty days late, seriously discuss payment or take legal action. Discuss a workout with interest. In no instance should you wait more than thirty days past the due date without a clear understanding of the collection methods you plan to utilize. If the customer still does not respond, have an attorney on hand who can write a collection letter. As a *last* resort, employ a collection agency. (This will cost you between 30 and 50 percent of the value of the receivable.)

Often customers who cannot pay will take refuge in attempting to degrade or say that the product is faulty. How do you differentiate between an honest complaint and an attempt to avoid payment? The person with a legitimate complaint will usually file it immediately, while the one who is trying to avoid payment will wait until his bill is past due before complaining.

One division of mine typically had delinquent customers who raised this type of smokescreen. The way we resolved the issue was by going in and reclaiming the equipment on our lien. This equipment happened to be essential to the customers' operation, and it was amazing how many payments we received right before we went in to claim the equipment.

I don't want to mislead you. With friendly reminders and due diligence, most customers will pay their bills on time. But there are those who constantly attempt to operate on your money, and since you are in trouble, you need cash flow. Just remember that in a $12-million-in-annual-revenue business, each day of overdue collectibles removes $33,000 from your cash flow and costs you at a 12 percent interest rate $3,500 in *annual interest*. Then if you have average day's receivables of forty-five days versus normal collectibles of thirty days, that extra fifteen days removes $500,000 from your cash flow and costs you approximately $50,000 a year in interest.

A major campaign to get receivables down to acceptable levels is part of a major program to increase cash flow.

Even if you discount your receivables to a bank (this is an unbelievably costly method of obtaining cash), there is usually a provision for recourse of the loan amount back to you if there is nonpayment.

Inventory—The Burial Ground

We have already had an extensive discussion of inventory and the steps necessary to get it to turn, to obtain immediate control, to cut back on inventory, and to stop theft. These were all short-term measures to get inventory back to manageable levels. The question that eventually must be answered is: What do you do on a continuous basis to ensure that inventory remains under control on a long-term basis?

The keys to this answer are:

- Forecasting
- Purchasing and standardization
- Materials control

Financial Analysis: No-Bull Numbers

First of all, all inventory control systems will fail if you have lousy forecasts of usage, especially in a cyclical business. This means that *your sales department must be responsible for forecasts of usage by item.* Your sales manager will tell you this is impossible; all sales managers for some reason shy away from forecasts like the plague. The reason for this reaction is that a sales forecast represents a commitment on their part, and none of us likes to be pinned down on a hard-numbers basis. You *must* get hard numbers on a *monthly* basis at worst, and your production people must agree to them.

The best way to do this is to schedule a meeting once a month between your sales and production planning people to determine what production will be for the forthcoming months.

I used to use a rolling forecast for six months with the current month being cast in concrete, the following month softer, and so on. Each month we would add a month to the end and drop the month at the beginning. The forecast document would look like the table on the following page.

By involving sales in this process, a sense of commitment is obtained on both sales' and manufacturing's part. The key number is the available inventory as compared with targeted inventory.

Once this monthly rolling forecast is established, purchasing can do its job, by buying at the lowest possible price for your needs. Purchasing's role becomes more important as the material content of your product goes up. (So what else is new?) Many companies place a person in purchasing and then forget about him. I feel that the purchasing job should be held by the brightest, most ambitious person in the organization and should be turned over every two years so that the purchasing person is not tempted to become too comfortable with one or two suppliers.

TURNAROUND

FORECAST FOR THE MONTH OF ——— THROUGH ———

UNITS

PRODUCT	CURRENT INVENTORY	COMMITTED BOOKED NOT SHIPPED	AVAILABLE INVENTORY	SALES/PRODUCTION BY MONTH			
				+1	+2	+3	+4
Widget	300	100	200	500/400	400/400	300/350	300/350

Approved: Production Manager ———

Sales Manager ———

In addition to the preceding position, a materials control function must be fulfilled. The person who holds this job coordinates the forecasting, production planning, purchasing, and product-engineering functions to ensure that parts are standardized wherever possible, that optimum quantities of supplies are purchased, and that incoming quality and quantities are controlled adequately. This person is your traffic cop and should be a materials control specialist with a heavy background in computers.

Here's a horror story of what can happen to you if you don't watch out: A company I know, which shall remain nameless, was producing a series of products; in fact, it had more than five hundred line items in its catalogue with no standardization. The way this happened was that each time the Engineering Department designed a new product, it started from scratch and did not consider parts that it was already buying. Therefore, a new set of screws was specified every time a new product was introduced, although functionally several hundred types of screws were already being purchased for existing products that met exactly the same functional need. The proliferation of parts became so great that there were at one point more than eighteen thousand line items of parts to support the five hundred products. The cost in space, inventory, and obsolescence was astronomical. *Don't let this happen to your company.*

Reserves

Watch out; here come the alligators. Most people think that reserves are a toy of the accountants and don't relate to the real world. You must watch out for these alligators when you acquire a company, turn a company around, or sell a company because these beasts can eat the ownership or you personally.

Let's talk about some of these alligators:

Reserves for Unpaid Taxes

If employee FICA or federal estimated taxes have not been paid or employee withholding taxes are not paid, you as an officer of the company and the directors are *personally* liable. These represent net cash flow liabilities that *must be paid*.

Pension Funds

Under ERISA, pension funds are supposed to be fully funded; that is, every employee's pension fund must have enough *assets on hand* to fund the transfer of that fund to another employer or retirement, if vested.

However, if the fund is older than the current regulations, a company has up to thirty years to fund the pension. This means that, if you acquire a company, the unfunded pension liability could be in the millions of dollars. Again, guess who could take it on the chin personally? That's right—the officers and the directors.

The best way to handle pension funds is to contact a specialist in the area of funds management. Shop among several specialists to determine the return on the fund, and the administrative charges, then place the funds with the best specialist you can find. The same philosophy is true with employee funds of any sort. The best way to manage these is to pick an employee committee to manage the picnic fund, the Christmas party fund, etc., with a member of management to act as an advisor.

Get these kinds of things completely out of the company's hands, since they spell nothing but potential trouble for you. One thing I have done is to help the employees establish a fund to cover parties, etc., with its own bank account. The company's cut of the vending machine proceeds in their totality are contributed to the fund, or the company agrees to match employee contributions for a party, such as the Christmas or spring picnic. You can really come off looking like a hero in this mode.

Legal Reserves (Who Sues Whom?)

Legal reserves can work both for you and against you. A legal reserve is a reserve that anticipates the results of a lawsuit that has been filed against the company and can result in a major loss to the corporation. Let's take both sides of the fence:

Advantages

A legal reserve can be established that reflects pending legal action, reduces current earnings on the profit-and-loss statement, and hence reduces tax liability. The extent of such reductions should be discussed with your tax attorney, but it provides a legal (excuse the play on words) method of reducing income in anticipation of an event. This reduction in turn increases current cash flow.

On the other hand, if you are grooming a company for sale legal reserves call attention to pending lawsuits, and even though you may reveal in your legal files that you have a potential liability, you don't call it out in the same manner that a reserve does.

Disadvantages

When acquiring a company, you must watch out for unreserved legal liabilities or an understatement of the potential cost of these liabilities when finally resolved. Legal reserves and legal action should act as a flag for you to investigate the potential liability with your *own* attorney. Don't trust the *seller's figure*. Remember, litigation is described as a process in which both of the litigants enter as pigs and emerge as sausages.

Warranty Reserves—Now the Fun Begins!

Hoo! Boy, have I got a story for you. I once was involved with a company that had been sold to my corporation. The company manufactured a product that was warranted for ten years (five years unconditionally and five years on a declining basis). Some three years before the sale, the company had changed the process for manufacturing a major component of the product, and major problems had begun to show up fairly quickly. But it was over two years before the old owners reacted and changed the manufacturing process and almost three years before the problem was solved.

Meanwhile, sales had been growing at significant rates. Upon acquisition the company examined the liability reserve, and in line with liability experience the reserve appeared adequate. What the company failed to realize is that it had a ten-year time bomb built into the system. Fortunately in this instance, part of the payment for the company was made on a deferred basis so that the reserve could be adjusted to reflect the experience. However, the liability was approaching $1 million annually or 1 percent of sales and 10 percent of net profit before taxes. This was a killer.

A second phenomenon occurred as a result of these warranty claims. The competition started utilizing this weakness as a selling tool against the company. The company personnel became so sensitized to the faulty workmanship that they started giving credits for almost any problem without questioning the nature of those credits and, as a result, began increasing the company's outflow of cash.

Now you ask, "OK, I'm stuck with a warranty policy that is lousy. What can I do about it?"

Your warranty policy must reflect your experience with your product and competitive warranties within your industry. Realizing that no one is perfect, I would shoot for a combination of quality standards and warranty rates that results in a return level of between .1 percent and .3 percent and better if you can get it. Japanese firms achieve rates that are much lower than this on a regular basis. Methodology should be as follows:

1. Solve the basic problem. The first thing to do is correct the problem that is causing the warranty expense. Correct the quality problem, modify the process, but do whatever is necessary to solve the problem. If you don't have the internal expertise to accomplish this, hire an outside engineering firm to solve it for you, but *move on it immediately.*
2. Change your warranty policy to reflect industry standards. This doesn't solve past problems, but it may limit future ones. Have a study made of competitive warranties and decide where you wish to fall. Since you have a problem, you most likely do not want to have the most liberal warranty until you assure yourself that your problem has been solved. You can increase the warranty later.
3. If the "we're having problems, so give the store away" syndrome exists within your company, clamp approval controls on returns. In other words, make higher-level people in the company approve returns. In fact, in the company I described, the president made it mandatory that any return over $1,000 be signed by him.
4. Advertise the new process you are utilizing to "improve" your product through **PR**, direct mail, media, etc. Turn a disadvantage to your advantage.
5. Promote the "new quality image" with your own people and factory personnel through meetings, etc.

(More will be mentioned about this method later.)
6. On a spot basis, examine defective merchandise to determine whether the returns are caused by manufacturing problems or abuse.
7. In some instances, it is not economical to have the goods returned to the factory for rework. In these cases, have your sales personnel verify quantities, type of defect, and destruction of faulty merchandise in the customer's premises.
8. Often you can return reworked merchandise to the system as "seconds" on an unbranded basis or recover parts.

An extreme example of the method is a company that had such a severe warranty problem that it folded and could be purchased by accepting $3 million to cover the warranty liability. Of course, upon investigation it was easily determined that the true liability was more like $6 million, and there were no takers.

PROFIT-AND-LOSS STATEMENT (P&L) ITEMS: "LADIES AND GENTLEMEN, YOU WILL NOTICE THAT AT NO TIME DO MY HANDS LEAVE MY WRIST."

Basic Philosophy

I want to discuss basic philosophy with you once more before we enter the area of P&Ls. A good financial manager can make the P&L look almost any way that he wishes by exercising the latitudes available to him in the areas of reserves, chargeable expenses, and work-in-process valuation. The basic question is, does the company wish to maximize cash flow or maximize P&L

Financial Analysis: No-Bull Numbers 59

impact? The cash flow maximization principle will usually result in a tax minimization philosophy. The P&L maximization philosophy will result in greater earnings at the end of the year and hence a larger tax bill.

Let's look at where the two philosophies are used:

SITUATION	CASH FLOW MAXIMIZATION	P&L MAXIMIZATION
Corporation Traded Publicly (Earnings Per Share Basis)	No	Yes
Privately Held or Closely Held Corporation or Entrepreneurship	Yes	No
Grooming Company for Sale	No	Yes
Company with Cash Flow Problems *(in extremis)*	Yes	No
Grooming Company to Go Public	No	Yes
Division of Large Company	Rarely	Usually

There are other situations and circumstances that I haven't covered but you get the idea. You must keep your financial objectives in mind at all times when operating a company. Let's take some examples:

SITUATION	CASH FLOW MAXIMIZATION	P&L MAXIMIZATION
Reserves	Yes	No
Accelerated Depreciation	Yes	No
Lease vs. Buy*	Yes (short-term) No (long-term)	Yes (short-term) No (long-term)
Obsolete Equipment and Supplies Write-off	Rapid	Measured
Inventory Valuation Method (during inflation)	LIFO	FIFO
Inventory Valuation Method (during deflation)	FIFO	LIFO
Large Executive Perks	Yes**	No
Deferred Compensation Programs	Yes	Yes
Other Tax Deferral Methods	Yes	Yes

* NOTE: Each lease situation should be studied on an individual basis based on alternative values of cash to you and the leasing company and the speed of technical obsolescence of the equipment leased.
** This increases the cash flow to the ownership, not necessarily to the corporation.

Sit down with your controller and impress him with the philosophy that you have decided on and then obtain further ideas from him.

Financial Analysis: No-Bull Numbers

Now let's get to P&L items and specific expenses we have discussed—SIB (short-interval budgeting).

Each business has its key items of expense that characterize it. You already know what they are; you just haven't focused on them. Since this book is dedicated to turnarounds, I presume that you have precious little time to devote to areas that have little impact on performance. The old 80/20 rule applies: 20 percent of the expense categories cause 80 percent of the expenses, so scan your P&L and write down the expense items that characterize your business.

Let me give you some examples of businesses that are clear-cut:

BUSINESS	KEY EXPENSE ITEMS
Services	Compensation, Benefits, T&E, Rent
Airlines	Compensation, Benefits, Money Costs
Chemical and Oil Companies	Raw Materials, Energy, Money Costs
Insurance Companies	Claims, Interest on Facilities and Computers, Compensation and Benefits, T&E
Utilities	Raw Energy Sources, Money Costs, Compensation and Benefits
Manufacturing	Raw Materials, Energy (sometimes), Compensation (sometimes), T&E
Drug Companies	R&D (people and facilities), Advertising and Promotion, Legal and Governmental, Quality Control (compensation and facilities)

I would suggest that you take your annual P&L and circle the items that are your greatest cost items. Then calculate the percentage they are of gross sales and enter the percentage on a form that looks like that on the following page.

Now remember, I told you to be sure to get as much financial information on your competitors as possible. The reason is that I now want you to list your competitors' expenses as a percentage of gross sales. Of course, the amounts for each of your competitors will not always be available, but enter what you can glean from the annual reports and 10Ks.

Of course, it doesn't necessarily follow that, if your percentages in a given expense area are low, you are operating at better levels than your competitors or even efficiently as compared with other businesses. However, this comparison does give you a reference point.

The problem with most managers, when it comes to expenses, is that they have no idea what the proper level of expense should be in any given category, so they use historical data from their own company. What this practice leads to is perpetuation of the same old mistakes. It's like the government. We all know that within the U.S. government there are departments whose purpose for existence has long faded into the mists of time. These departments continue to live because Congress has neither the time nor the awareness of the function in order to dismantle them. It is amazing how many things we do because "it's always been done that way," and the larger the corporation, the more of these types of things exist. OK, so let's examine each area. Because of the topic's complexity, I'm going to devote a whole chapter later in the book to manufacturing costs, so let's discuss other kinds of cost first.

EXPENSE ITEMS' PERCENTAGE OF GROSS SALES

GROSS SALES (GS) $ ⎯⎯⎯ EXPENSE ITEMS	% OF GS	% OF GS COMPETITOR #1	% OF GS COMPETITOR #2	% OF GS COMPETITOR #3
Compensation				
Benefits				
Material				
Energy				
T&E				
R&D/Engineering				

Freight In and Out: "Why is my trucker in Walla Walla?"

If you are selling a product that is sold FOB your facilities or a service that does not involve freight, you are about to skip this section. *Don't.* First, everybody buys things, and it is important that you know how to minimize the cost of delivery of product to your door. Second, if you sell product FOB your plant, the freight cost becomes part of your selling price to the customer because any astute buyer examines product on a delivered cost basis. Anybody who has a plant on the East Coast and has tried to compete with a West Coast manufacturer for a customer who is located on the West Coast has first-hand experience with this fact.

Freight In

Let's look at freight in first. On products quoted on a delivered basis, there is a freight element that, although hidden, is present nevertheless. Most suppliers who quote in this manner have averaged their delivery costs across the nation over the price of the products, so that the company nearest the factory is subsidizing the company farthest away. Ways to get around this include the following:

- Ask if there is a discount if you pick up the product yourselves. (There usually is.)
- If you have trucks of your own, find out the incremental cost of a backhaul by diverting your returning trucks to your supplier.
- If you don't have trucks, find out if you can hire someone to haul your merchandise at costs below the discount level allowed by the manufacturer. Since the deregulation of trucking, this has become a very viable alternative.

Financial Analysis: No-Bull Numbers

In FOB deliveries to you by your suppliers, again examine what the supplier charges you versus what your own trucking costs or what a trucker that you choose would charge. Trucking companies you hire will give you a credit for lining up the backhaul.

Freight Out

Freight out is often a significant cost for a company. Depending on the product, it can be 5 percent of the selling price of the item when you include insurance, maintenance, and other associated costs. To gain control of your trucking costs, you have to ask those who operate in this area a number of questions. You break down these questions as follows.

For those who own or lease their own fleet (lucky you):

- "Based on the cost of trucking and my distribution patterns, what are the optimum places I should ship in truckload quantities, and where should I warehouse and break bulk?" These questions alone can generate a report the size of the New York City telephone directory. There are experts in transportation analysis who can tell you the answers and optimize your savings utilizing a computer analysis of your current and projected sales patterns.
- "Are we utilizing our backhauls to the fullest?" You don't have to backhaul for only yourselves; you can also line up backhauls of products to your area for others. Again, because of the relaxation of regulations, your company can act as an independent common carrier and often can offset its outbound freight costs with this approach.
- "Are we running our freight function as a business with the same safeguards as any prudently run business?" I won't go into the litany of problems

ranging from theft, to truckers going many miles off their route to see a girlfriend, to overcharges on company gasoline credit cards, etc. These problems can all be avoided by operating the shipping function crisply and efficiently.

For those who do not own their own fleet or are shipping FOB (lucky you):

As previously stated, the first two points above apply also to those who don't own their own fleets and can generate large volumes of shipments. In addition, the following questions can also be asked for the company that buys shipping services.

- "What rebates are available to me if I use one shipping company in volume?" Shippers are now granting cash rebates to shippers who utilize them for a major portion of their shipping business. These rebates can be in the thousands of dollars per month, depending on your shipping volume. This rebate applies to companies who add freight charges to their bills.
- "Can I add a handling charge for my internal shipping control and have it covered in my FOB shipments?"
- "What alternate shipping methods are there to truck and rail?"

You may laugh at this last question, but it may be cheaper for you to ship to the West Coast or vice versa, via shipping through the Panama Canal, than to ship cross-country via rail or truck. Examine all the alternatives. Many companies ship in less than truckload quantities more often than they know, and the cost of these types of shipments is enormous because the same driver, the same gas, the same wear and tear exist for a delivery no matter how full the truck is. So the optimum situation is to ship *only full truckloads*. This, of course, is unrealistic, so what do you do? The answer is to upcharge the price significantly for less than truckload shipments and to ship full truckloads to warehouses and then to ship smaller trucks from there.

As part of your trucking analysis, you should ask for an analysis of the percentage each truck is full when it leaves the plant. I guarantee that you will be shocked.

Demurrage: "Take your time; it's only costing us money."

Demurrage is the amount you pay extra for holding any transportation beyond normal off-loading times. This can vary from $35 a day for a containerized shipment to $50,000 a day for a tanker. I would like to relate a personal experience regarding demurrage.

I was executive vice president of an independent oil company, and part of my responsibilities extended to a refinery in Louisiana. We did not own our own terminal but rather leased from a large terminal firm. I noted when I took over the refinery operations that demurrage was $250,000 per month, and that was just one of several major problems we had. Needless to say, this figure was staggering.

The following night a ship was due into the dock at 2:00 A.M., and I wanted to see how off-loading was handled. I waited at the pier for the ship to come up the channel, and it finally appeared at 4:00 A.M. (two hours past due). The unloading crew had been dismissed by this time, and the ship sat offshore for five hours until someone decided to tie the ship up to the pier. Since the terminal crew was busy with other things, the ship was not hooked up to the hoses until the following evening, and after some shifting around of product and determination of where the crude oil should go, the off-loading began. The clock on demurrage had begun, however, the moment the ship had arrived at our dock, at the rate of $12,000 a day.

Now that I knew what the problem was, I arranged to meet with the captain of the next ship that came in and asked him how we might speed up the process of off-loading. He indicated to me that the ship, of course, had radio gear, and he could estimate very closely, once he entered the ship channel, how long it would be before he reached our docks. If we had a radio call frequency, he and others could accurately indicate their arrival time and cargo so that the proper lines and tanks could be prepared for the transfer in advance.

I immediately purchased a radio and designated a round-the-clock shipping coordination team. I also made the terminal management aware of our requirements for rapid turnaround of ships and asked for their cooperation in the matter. In addition, I suggested that they would participate in the demurrage costs if such levels of turnaround could not be achieved.

In fact, they were more than helpful in organizing the effort with us. Within three days our demurrage dropped from $250,000 per month to *zero*. The cost of the three-shift shipping coordination operation was around $100,000 per year, *a savings of $2.9 million* a year, and it was accomplished in *three days*.

The moral of all this is that, through a commonsense examination of shipping costs, some real plums can be plucked. However, in the example that I have given you, it was the financial documents that led me to the problem, and it was common sense and a little advice from those involved in the problem that generated the solution.

To Own, Lease, or Use Common Carriers

One of the questions I perhaps should have answered in the beginning of this section is how you determine whether you should own your own transportation, lease it, or use common carriers. The answer to this question is "I don't know," so I avoided the question altogether. The answer depends greatly on each individual case and where you are located. The transportation expert you hire to determine your optimum distribution pattern can give you the answer based on your products, your sales patterns, your shipping volume, the location of your shipping facilities, the amount of control you desire, the labor environment in your area, and the cash you have available for the fleet investment. Under the current deregulation of trucking, it is becoming harder and harder to justify an "in-house" fleet on a financial basis.

Freight Damage

The last area I want to discuss regarding common carriers is freight damage. I feel that corporations in the United States lose millions of dollars a year as a result of unclaimed or disallowed freight damages.

A great way to save many, many dollars is by insisting that your customers inspect goods and report freight damage while the trucker is still in the plant and not sign for short shipments that are not indicated as such on the bill of lading. Many receiving clerks sign receiving slips without ever counting or examining the goods, and several weeks later, when they finally get around to it, they find shortages or damage. Then the manufacturer gets a return with no way of ascertaining who did it.

This procedure can be enforced through a "you sign for it, you own it" policy. This policy is harsh but is the only way of placing a creditable claim on the trucker for damaged or misplaced goods. And I am sure that your customer will understand because he faces the same kind of problem. There are also a few unscrupulous customers who claim short shipments "after the fact" and who really haven't been shorted.

Operating Expenses: "Don't touch my expenses; they're just fine."

Compensation: "I need all my people."

I am a great advocate of zero-based budgeting and rejustifying staff each year. I think it morally wrong to pay a lot of people poorly to keep them employed in functions in which they are not productive, rather than paying a few people who do well handsomely. Too many companies in the United States settle for mediocre and disinterested performance because they expect too little from their people and pay accordingly.

Every successful entrepreneurial operation is thin on staff and overworked and usually has happy people. In Chapter 5 I will discuss people and how I feel you should motivate them to achieve maximum productivity and fun out of the job, so let's not discuss that now. Let's talk about positions and staffing.

You should list *all* the positions in your organization and then answer the following questions without regard for the personality filling that position:

"What does the position do?"
"Can that position be combined with another one for a one-person reduction?"
"What alternatives are there to staffing this position in terms of part-time or outside help?"
"What would the company economically gain or lose as a result of this position being staffed?"
"What are our future plans, and how does this position relate to them?"

This analysis should be done for *every* job in the company and in written format.

In the United States, the equation, *manager + size of staff = amount of power* is the driving force in most companies. We are all, without exception, empire builders, and most of us are driven by the ability and desire to manipulate others. This motivation is not necessarily bad, but it becomes destructive when it causes staff to grow beyond the means of an operation to support it.

In doing the preceding type of annual restaffing exercise, you will become absolutely amazed by how many positions you can do without and still accomplish your objectives. In troubled companies you will find that jobs and fancy titles have had a tendency to proliferate because, as the businy economically gain or lose as a result of this position being staffed?"

I will discuss productivity as it relates to function elsewhere. Suffice it to say here that this initial exercise will help trim down staff considerably.

Getting Control of Personal Expenses: "Doesn't everyone travel first class?"
Travel and Entertainment

I always have been an advocate of not scrutinizing expense accounts closely because if I feel someone is cheating on his expense account he shouldn't be working for me. However, I feel strongly about placing general controls on expenses so that scrutiny is not necessary. Let's discuss the items on the expense account and how you control and reduce them.

Travel Justification. I have my people justify their travel to their supervisor in writing and obtain his approval for such travel in writing. Here are the key questions that you should ask in these instances:

1. Is the travel really necessary, or is it something that could be handled by phone or telex? (This should be a matter of discussion between the traveler and supervisor.)
2. If travel is necessary, can the individual traveling perform another task while in the area? (This should be formalized by posting a schedule of where people are traveling the week before they go so that others can ask them to handle items for them. This also helps develop a "team" spirit within the organization, since it demands that people assist each other in an interdisciplinary manner.)

Travel. The cost of airfares and transport is rising rapidly, and the only way to beat the game is to travel at the lowest fare possible. There are special fares available, and I would insist that all airline business be booked through one travel agent who, in turn, always seeks the lowest fares possible for corporate personnel. I have always traveled at the lowest fare possible because I felt that it is difficult to demand frugality on the part of your people when you are unwilling to exercise it yourself. In those rare instances in which I was in need of more spacious accommodations, I would pay for the cost myself. I visualize the day when there will be corporate-rate airfares, but until then, this system works fairly well.

Autos. What I have done is to pick one or two auto rental companies and develop master agreements with them for corporate rates on the smallest cars they offer. Again, the boss travels the same way the troops do.

Hotels. I have managed to pick several hotel chains and develop corporate rates and upgrade programs, which are quite attractive, with them. Most of the major hotel chains are willing to negotiate if you are willing to send them a large portion of your business. In addition, most chains have individual "gold" cards that allow your people some "special treatment" that recognizes them as frequent travelers. Significant savings can be garnered in this way.

Entertainment. This is the most difficult area to control. Most traveling people view this as a perk associated with the unpleasantness of travel and hence will entertain lavishly. There are two ways to handle entertainment expenses: First, establish a policy statement for all personnel who travel and set forth guidelines as to the type of entertainment that is allowable. Second, budgeting of travel and entertainment on a monthly basis makes traveling individuals comply with the guidelines but allows them the discretion of where to spend their funds.

I have seen corporate personnel drinking themselves into a stupor while on the road, destroying their health, and costing their companies thousands of dollars in both ineffective performance and outlays for booze. In today's business environment, you can't afford this type of person. You need a "pull together" type of spirit, and all hands have to help in reducing costs, whether they are under the scrutiny of the corporation or operating independently.

4
ANALYZING THE P&L AND FINDING OUT WHERE IT GOES
Some Personal Experiences— Item-by-Item Analysis

Earlier I had you study each cost item on your P&L to determine what part of sales it represents. You now have each item as a percentage of sales and some idea of what your competitions' cost structure is.

LONG-TERM P&L ANALYSIS

The objective now is to attack each P&L item on a long-term basis. The examples below are the kinds of things that can be done through an item-by-item analysis. You must take the same approach for each and every item in tedious detail and, with the perseverance of a

Sherlock Holmes, ferret out the reasons for expenses and the alternative approaches available.

Telephone and Telegraph: "Let's call Mom after hours."

The eventual aim is to reduce the cost of this item on a permanent basis. Toward that end, here are just a few questions you can ask:

What is this cost?
What is the nature of our outgoing calls?
Are we accepting too many incoming calls?
Who has access to our outgoing lines?
Would a WATS system save us money?
Do we have too many telephones for our needs?

Once you have determined the answers to such questions, make, in writing, assignments for their resolution and positive suggestions as to their solution. There are innovative ways to reduce telephone and telex costs without impairing business. Set a definite time schedule for return of the analysis and indicate where the investigator can turn for assistance and ideas.

Here, as in other areas, I have used the management committee approach to provide new inputs and ideas for reducing costs.

Energy Costs: "Leave the lights on; it doesn't cost much."

Ask these types of questions:

What items are causing the majority of our costs?
What are substitute sources of energy and their relative cost?
Can we shut down parts of our energy-using opera-

Analyzing the P&L

tions in off-peak hours and shift operations to other areas?
Can we shift high-electrical load operations to off-peak hours to lower our power factor?
Can we shop for a "better" fuel oil deal?
Can we use computerized energy management techniques?
Can we employ an energy bill management consultant to examine our utility bills to determine if we have overpaid? (These consultants are people who come in and examine your utility bills to see if you are paying the proper rates. They normally split any savings they obtain with you.)

Operating Supplies: "Yes, I take paper home for the kids; so what?"

Some questions to ask on this item are:

Are we wasting supplies?
What are we buying and why?
What is our consumption of supplies, and why is it so high?
Are we wasting materials or losing items through white-collar theft?

Lease/Rental Payments

Ask questions like these:

Have we made proper lease/buy determinations?
Do we need to lease certain types of equipment?
What alternatives exist?

I recently was faced with the choice of renting some office furniture or purchasing it. An examination of the rent/buy options indicated to me that the cost of renting was so high that I would have paid back the cost of a purchase in three months. Because of cash flow problems, I decided to buy the furniture through a third-party lessor on a long-term (five-year) lease. The cost was higher than purchase but much lower than a rental.

Also, reexamine your space rental costs. Often a heart-to-heart discussion with your landlord, after you have studied the availability of alternate quarters and their costs, as well as the cost of a move, can be beneficial. You can often negotiate a lower rate if you are willing to commit to a longer lease period. It might also be advisable to move to smaller quarters if your business has contracted. *Do not view this as a sign of defeat;* it is merely a retrenchment.

This is also the time to get rid of unprofitable facilities and the burdens that they carry with them.

OTHER AREAS TO ANALYZE

General and Administrative Costs: "It doesn't fit anywhere else; let's put it in G&A."

G&A becomes the dumping ground for the excesses of the corporation. Often because G&A is generally allocated across many divisions or entities, no one person feels responsible for this cost. G&A contains the allocation for the chairman's toy, the corporate aircraft, someone's promise (a job for life in a staff position) to his brother Lou, or the president's favorite charity—the home for wayward racehorses. The following key questions should be asked in a turnaround:

Do we really need it?
Is it essential for the operation of the company?
If not, how do we get rid of it?

Staff people tend to forget that they are part of the P&L

as well and that they must make a contribution in order to exist. At the management committee meetings, there *are no sacred cows* if there is to be a true renewal. Therefore, the G&A expenses should be able to bear the brunt of the searchlight and the scrutiny of the operating staff.

You usually don't have to tell the operating staff that this opportunity exists more than one time, because they have been dying to "get" those guys in the front office for some time. Once the vitriol has abated, some darn good suggestions can often come out of such scrutiny. For example, dispose of the corporate aircraft, assimilate several corporate functions into one more meaningful one, or expose nonfunctional areas that are costing a great deal.

The idea is to get a series of positive long-term action plans that result in profitability for each division. This might involve spending money to make money, but the scrutiny is the important factor.

Taxes: "I'm from Washington and here to help you!"

A controllable expense, believe it or not, is taxes. Taxes, since corporate tax rates are a high percentage of your gross income, are perhaps your largest single expense. They should be treated with the respect and scrutiny you would accord any expense of this magnitude.

This is the place where you should utilize tax experts either as consultants or as employees to lay out a tax strategy that legally minimizes the corporate outlay for taxes. Most companies do not take advantage of all the legal opportunities available to them for reduction in taxes or deferment of taxes.

An example of this situation was an opportunity that presented itself for the movement of a facility to a tax haven. The government had decreed that we separate two facilities we owned. (This was regulatory in nature and related to the products made in those two facilities.) The following question was then asked of me: "How can we separate these two facilities and realize some offset in cost because of tax or labor incentives?" Since the move would be costly, I proceeded to investigate various local tax havens, local grants, etc., and came up with Puerto Rico as the number one choice.

We had a high-value, small-sized product that was easily transportable, and Puerto Rico was heavily involved in an industrial incentive program that granted a federal tax haven under Section 931 of the Internal Revenue Code. (Compliance with the current code is much more complex than I have time to indicate here, and I'm providing the example for illustrative purposes only.) The result was the establishment of a manufacturing facility in Puerto Rico that paid for itself in tax relief in less than one year and continued to generate extremely high returns for the following ten years (the period of the tax relief). There were certain other offsetting factors as to liberation of funds back to the United States, the amount of value added in public relations, restrictions as to investment of the cash generated, etc. However, the approach was most advantageous.

There are many items like this that provide tax relief if employed judiciously and properly. I read that the average annual true payment of taxes by U.S. businesses was only 12 percent of gross income as the result of items such as this example, tax loss carry forwards, etc.

It is worthwhile having a tax expert examine your statements to ascertain your ability to reduce your tax burden by some judicious planning, especially if you plan on making an acquisition or moving facilities or making *any major investment*.

This effort should be begun in parallel with other

activities since, if you are successful in your activities, you will maximize cash flow by minimizing tax outlays.

REVIEWS—WHEN AND HOW OFTEN?

In a renewal there should be a period of very intense reviews with your management group. For example, meeting every day for one hour in the morning and for a number of hours on Monday is not unheard of. If holding so many meetings puts too much stress on the staff, then evening meetings, say from 6:00 to 8:00 P.M., are called for. Remember, you are trying to improve profitability fast, and intense activity is required. Once tasks are assigned, you can cut your meetings to twice a week and then, finally, to once a week.

In a troubled company, I would not anticipate getting down to once-a-week meetings for at least a year or until turnaround is achieved. But in a pure renewal situation, a once-a-week schedule can come very quickly.

You can allow certain personnel to be absent from business meetings, etc., during the week but *never* from your key Monday meetings. If any personnel protest, tell them to plan around it. Some experts have used Saturdays as their meeting day. Although I don't advocate that, it certainly brings home the message of the seriousness of the effort and has the advantage of freeing people from the numerous telephone calls and other interruptions that occur during the week. Soon (usually about the second week), if you insist on perfect attendance at the Monday meetings, you will hear, "I can't do anything because I am always in meetings." The way to quash this objection is immediately to move to evening meetings or break-of-dawn meetings. Soon the staff will realize the discretion of not bringing up "old saws" regarding meetings.

Each meeting should result in an action list or additions or subtractions from old action lists and an indication of who is doing what. Therefore, a secretary (usually yours) should take notes. I have tried having one or more of the participants be the secretary, and this approach does not work because personal biases appear in the minutes and differences in formats creep in. So do it yourself or through your secretary. Or if you have a corporate planner, have him prepare the notes and action plan.

Now that you have the modus operandi for cleaning up the P&L, I would like to move to perhaps the most difficult and most rewarding task associated with a renewal; that is, converting a nonproductive or marginally productive work force into a happy, productive one.

5
PEOPLE
Love 'Em or Leave 'Em

In earlier chapters I said that in the renewal effort you will be rejustifying positions, cutting costs, and examining each cent spent. Now how do you do this without causing morale problems among the work force? This issue is a legitimate concern, but if handled properly it can not only positively affect your work force but improve morale as well.

BASIC PHILOSOPHY

I *truly* believe that people are your most important asset and can be your greatest liability as well. All the plans, action steps, deliberations, etc., generated in previous chapters and forthcoming chapters in this book are meaningless without the proper people to carry out the action plans. It is people who can carry a company from the brink of failure to great success, and it is also people who can snatch defeat from the jaws of victory.

A poor manager can create an atmosphere of defensiveness and poor performance that can permeate his entire organization. If I had the space, I could relate to you how many thousands of times I have heard, "That wasn't my responsibility," or "They did it the wrong way," or "That was their fault." Oh, there have been good stretches of time when my being has ached for the honesty of the words "Yes, I made a mistake, but I learned not to do it again," or "I tried and failed, but I'm going to try again," or "Here's where we went wrong; let's try it this way."

It is so important that the right attitude be developed during a renewal that I am going to spend some time discussing attitude in this chapter.

In the beginning, I stated that a renewal is of *necessity* a *benevolent dictatorship*. However, I don't want you to develop a group of yes-people. The idea is to create a constructive atmosphere in which new ideas can be developed without fear of ridicule. Three keys to achieving this atmosphere are:

- The interview technique I earlier asked you to utilize
- The management committee approach to problem solving
- A constant communication link between you and *all* the people in the organization

You wish to extend yourself, not to *clone* yourself.

No matter how good your company is, you are going to end up with some bad actors—people who hang tenaciously on to their jobs because they can't do anything else, those who are so inefficient that they know they might have to really work somewhere else, or the poor souls who are just in jobs that are way beyond their ability. Whatever the reason, you will have to fire some people. Again, remember it is better to remove a few inefficient people than to make many suffer for the actions of a few.

Another thing I demand from people is that I must be able to trust implicitly what they say to me. I once told my petty officers in the Navy that I never had a petty officer lie to me because, once they had, they weren't petty officers any longer.

The same thing is true in a renewal. You cannot be burdened with sorting fact from fiction, half-truths, or lies. This precept must be made clear to your personnel, and especially your managers, immediately. In turn, you must be absolutely honest with your people and straightforward in your relationships with them.

The Open-Door Policy

I said above that one of the keys to establishing a constructive atmosphere is keeping in touch and communicating with your people. To make a renewal successful, the lowest-ranking individual within the organization must be able to have access to the highest level in the company without fear of recrimination or derision. By this I mean an open-door policy. This means that any individual who has fears, apprehension, etc., about his job or anything else that is happening in the company can, by request, move through the chain of management to the president's office to get questions answered or grievances heard. This process should take no more than forty-eight hours.

Your response to this, if you're the president, undoubtedly will be "My God, I'll be swamped." In all the years that I ran companies of various sizes—from several hundred employees to several thousand—I have had only between ten and twenty personal interviews, and those were to settle work-related grievances. In only one of those incidents did I find it necessary to reverse the decision of a subordinate, but in all of the instances some fair and equitable resolution of the problem that met our mutual need was developed. Some of the other communication techniques I have used will be enumerated later in this chapter.

Maximizing Output/Maximizing Fun

Up to now we have talked about all the steps and hard work necessary to achieve renewal, but now I want to talk about fun. It's no fun to be part of a marginally profitable or losing team. So it's time to put some fun back into the team's life, and the way to do it is to emphasize not the hard work, but rather the satisfaction that will come from the activity of renewal itself.

MODIFYING EMPLOYEES' ATTITUDES

It is difficult to impart in these pages the kinds of things you can do to modify attitudes because what is needed varies from place to place and situation to situation. There are, however, attitudes that you must communicate to your people directly to get them "in the spirit." Make sure they understand these facts:

- You are looking for solutions to problems.
- No creative solution to a problem will ever be

ridiculed. It is only the lack of innovative thinking that is to be avoided.
- In the renewal process, everyone is going to make mistakes. As long as the mistake is correctable, it is not serious.
- Progress is not made without risk.

These values, if imparted to your people, put them in the proper framework for attacking the problems of the business. And once the ideas start flowing and progress can be seen, you would be surprised at the change in attitude.

Once I have discussed the preceding approach with my people, I can no longer accept these responses: "They did it," or "That wasn't my area of responsibility." I always ask who "they" are and why there always has to be some remote, unnamed villain. *The solution to the problem is the central issue and placing blame has no importance.* This lesson will be drummed into your people many, many times because it goes against the basic corporate lesson of PYA (protecting your ass).

Now I have discussed attitude modification, which partially includes changing people's attitude toward work tasks and deadlines. Work tasks in a company merely represent another opportunity for employees to expose themselves to management's scrutiny. Therefore, often employees tend to avoid assignment completion at all costs and to try to ensure that results will be so ambiguous as to defy analysis.

I have seen grown men quake at the question "What are your specific recommendations?" In the renewal situation, you must make it clear that certain assignments are due by the deadline and no later because the progress of the renewal depends on each individual's completing his assignment. This means making clear, concise recommendations in a timely manner.

HANDLING EMPLOYEES WHO DON'T ACHIEVE THEIR GOALS

Now what do you do if certain people don't achieve the goals indicated? The answer is to determine why they can't do so, remove the perceived obstacles, and then insist that the goals be reached by an agreed-upon time (usually within an extremely short time frame). If you still don't get the output you want, reassign the task to someone else and consider reassigning the individuals originally responsible to job levels at which they can perform or removing them from the company. This is a difficult action to take, but nothing can stand in the way of other, more capable employees. Usually peer pressure will cause those who can't perform to leave the ship.

This brings us to the question of deadwood. I always believe that people deserve a chance to show their talents or lack of them. When people are really trying, I always try harder to find a spot for them at which they can attain maximum potential or to identify their weaknesses and help them overcome them. I cannot tolerate lazy people, and if a member of the staff is lazy or uncooperative, the scenario takes the following format:

1. Assignment of tasks
2. Failure to perform
3. Heart-to-heart talk in private
4. Failure to perform
5. Ultimatum
6. Failure to perform
7. Termination

I have made people work for me who had never had to

face the hard choice between performance and termination. These people tend to cruise through their jobs, doing the minimum amount necessary to survive. In the meantime, they are resented by others and demoralize those around them.

I had a man work for me who was holding down two jobs. His absenteeism record was extremely high (forty-five days of sick leave a year). His excuse was a bad back. I subsequently found out that he was working as a bartender at night, standing on his feet until all hours.

I summoned him to my office and informed him that I was about to uncomplicate his life for him and to solve his back problem. I told him he had a choice of staying in our Sales Department or making a career decision to become a bartender. I asked him to come to me with his decision. By the end of the day at 5:00 P.M., he came to my office and informed me that his only work activity would be as a member of our team.

I then told him to get his back taken care of and then return to work on a full-time basis. This man straightened out his act and became a very valuable employee. I later promoted him because of his enthusiasm and contributions to the company.

There are, however, others who, no matter what you do for them, will not alter their work patterns and will never perform as desired or expected. The only solution in these instances is a quick, merciful dismissal.

It is usually the shock that an individual needs to get his career back on track, and you clear the decks for those who will perform.

EVALUATING PERSONNEL TO CHOOSE A MANAGEMENT TEAM

The hardest thing you will have to do in a renewal is

evaluating performance and the people around you to determine who will be part of the eventual management team.

I usually like to look at what I would normally expect from a position on a functional basis and then analyze what I feel the incumbent has done in the position over the last several years. I also list what I feel will be expected from the position in the future and then again evaluate the incumbent against expectations to see if I feel that the individual in the job is up to future needs.

The way to do this analysis is to prepare a written job description and then compare how the incumbent fares against each requirement. You should do this with each of your key staff members and have them do the same with each of their key employees, and so on down the line, until all managers have been evaluated. Then a full review of all management personnel is made at the top levels of the company.

You must offer continuing and heartfelt praise and encouragement to those who do perform and pitch in during a renewal. People *must* be complimented when they do well.

I quite often would give parties for personnel when we reached specific goals or objectives that were attainable within relatively short time frames. For example, during the start-up of a production line, I promised the production line personnel and their managers a beer party, paid for by me personally, if their output reached a thousand units a day of good production. This output became a real goal for our plant people, and it took more than two months to reach it. But we all had a lot of fun cheering them on, and beer never tasted sweeter than when we reached the target.

I have also encouraged staff personnel with golf outings, picnics, poker nights, etc. When a manager, no matter what his or her level, performed extremely well, my wife and I would take the manager and spouse out to dinner.

The whole idea is to get everyone pulling together during the intensive activity required during a renewal and to recognize people for their efforts.

This recognition doesn't have to cost the company a great deal of money. It just has to provide the boost in ego we all need. In one company I gave turkeys to the employees at Thanksgiving and hams at Christmas. At other times we would have potluck luncheons to share with the other employees.

What I am saying by all this is that managing people properly is getting not only normal performance out of them but also a little something extra!

The first clue that you are succeeding in this goal is that people start coming in early and leaving late without being asked. This means that they are enjoying their jobs and want to contribute, no matter what the personal sacrifice.

REDUCTIONS IN WORK FORCE: "YOU MONSTER!"

It is never pleasant to fire anyone, but in a renewal it is inevitable that there will be fallout. Remember, I stated these two basic precepts in firing:

1. The greater good is always more important than any one person.
2. If done properly, a firing benefits both the party being fired and the company doing the firing.

It is important that you realize that a firing, unless for some form of malfeasance, need not be a "good-bye, you are out!" type of operation. Here are methods of softening the blow:

- Severance pay
- Allowing the severed party to utilize a company phone and secretarial help
- Use of an outplacement firm
- In the case of layoffs, establishment of an internal placement office
- Letters of recommendation (if justified)

These provisions are self-explanatory and provide the individual being separated with some dignity with which to seek and obtain another position.

If a firing is performed, the person being fired should be:

- Informed of the reasons for termination
- Informed of the services and severance that the company is willing to grant
- Given the time frame for evacuation of the premises (usually the sooner the better)
- Dismissed by the person to whom he reports, with someone from the Personnel Department present at the time

Some managers cannot fire people because their emotional structure does not allow them to. They shift the job to others or generally avoid unfavorable evaluations of subordinates because they can't be faced with eventual terminations. These people are not really managers because they will perpetuate mediocre performance because of their unwillingness to face unpleasant situations.

I have literally fired hundreds of people and shut down

many facilities, and it is never a pleasant task. The day I garner some sense of power from this unpleasant part of my job is the day I will give up what I am doing. However, in many instances the task needs to be done, and every manager must be prepared to do it. If I have made any one mistake in my career, it has been *waiting too long* to dismiss an incompetent employee.

The Valuable Work Force

When you work in Japan and you join a Japanese company, even today, you are virtually assured a sinecure for life, even at the lowest levels in the organization. Therefore, Japanese companies select their people very well and very carefully. They also motivate their people and explain the complex interrelationships of their job to overall corporate performance.

I have often thought it ridiculous that in American industry, when sales are down, we lay off a number of factory workers instead of firing the sales manager. The factory workers have absolutely nothing to do with sales being down, but they are laid off even when they have been turning in their best performance. In turn, when shoddy merchandise goes out, we often blame the salesperson for being unable to sell the product, instead of tracing the problem back to the plant. We Americans are an impatient lot, and we expect results instantaneously. So the first response to a downturn in sales is to lay off or fire people.

I am basically opposed to this practice and feel that the way to solve the problem, even in cyclical businesses, is to establish two levels of work force:

1. The first level consists of a cadre of talented people who provide your skills base. An individual earns his way into this exclusive club through effort, skill,

and loyalty, as do management personnel. This does not mean that these people are immune from replacement because of nonperformance. It does mean, however, that during economic downturns or cycles in the business these positions will be considered a "court of last resort" for reduction. Recognition of this status can be designated by calling a person a "member" or some other identifiable title giving certain privileges, such as profit sharing or other economic benefits, and creating a different feeling for these people.
2. The second level consists of those new entrants aspiring to join the "members" and attempting to prove their abilities and desire to remain a part of the organization. There should be an understanding with these people that in the event of cyclical reductions, etc., they may be laid off and that they will be judged fairly as to their worth and intent to become "members."

I feel that the number of "members" may vary as a company grows but should reflect the minimum work force under the worst of anticipated cyclical conditions.

The preceding solution does not relieve management of its responsibility for maintaining as level a production schedule as possible. It merely helps develop a feeling of belonging in a corporation.

In the initial phases of a renewal, it may be necessary to reduce a bloated work force to achieve optimum operating efficiency. It is imperative that you review each personnel decision (layoff or no layoff) by asking these questions:

Who is essential to the operation?
What is the optimum number of people for produc-

tion and sale of the product or operations at the desired quality standards?

What is the best way to reduce the work force—attrition, layoff, or firing?

In doing this review, you must identify key individuals and review each person's record, performance, and skills and the need for his talents.

Dealing with a Union

If you have a union, often the reduction of personnel is dictated by contractual constraints. In some instances, these can be modified through a discussion with the union officials to identify key graded jobs that cannot be replaced by bidding the jobs internally. Also, depending on the nature of the job, certain intermittent, key functions can be assumed by outside contractors if your bargaining agreement allows such action. Remember, the union is usually as interested in improving the company as you are and often will suggest productivity steps that can be made to improve output.

I must tell you that, in general, I am not enthusiastic about unions. The reason is the adversarial relationship that springs up between management and labor when a third party gets into the act. It becomes a "them" and "us" kind of relationship between the work force and management.

I feel that in a contemporary work environment the objectives of the employees and the employer are the same. There are enough economic and marketplace pressures today without two factions within the company (labor and management) facing off against each other.

My feeling is that, if I can manage a work force before a union gets into place, I will never have a union because I will treat my employees better than a union ever would be able to accomplish through adversarial negotiation.

Don't get me wrong. I feel that there is still a role for unions today. A union can serve largely as an educational and communicative or countervailing force in companies whose management is not enlightened. But with or without a union, management of personnel should generate a feeling of team spirit that pervades the entire organization.

So you say, "I have a union now. What do I do about it?" The answer is that you must enlist the union's aid in making the atmosphere in the company one of mutual, rather than diverse, objectives. In any renewal or turnaround, one of the first meetings should be with the union people to tell them what you are doing, what you are planning to do, and why.

If the union representative in your operation is worth his salt, he already knows the economic position of the company and some of the steps that need to be taken in your renewal effort.

The objective is to honestly enlist the union's aid in doing whatever will preserve jobs. This involves scheduling regular meetings with the union representatives to inform them of what is going on. Unions, like good managers, don't like surprises. A "team" approach can be tailored to include the union.

In one facility the union and the company for many years gave separate picnics and Christmas parties. After rapport was established with the union, a joint function was held. The union and the company split the cost, and the employees' committee planned the function.

Trust is built slowly, so don't expect to walk into the union hall and say, "OK, fellas, we're pals now. Let's dance."

I don't mean to suggest either that management has to

give up its rights or surrender to every union demand. The key here is fairness. You must treat employees as though there were no intervening organization such as a union.

Now, just as there are unscrupulous employers, there are unscrupulous unions. When you run into a situation of this type and you are in a turnaround, you have the following options:

- Shut down the troublesome operation and move its function into other existent facilities for economic reasons.
- Move the problem facility to where the economic situation is better.
- Be prepared to fight the gut issues with the union in contract negotiations (or to tolerate a work stoppage).

All these solutions involve making tough, hard decisions and must be evaluated on an economic basis alone. Emotion has no part in such decisions, both by law and for practical reasons, and the cost of each option must be considered. I have exercised one or more of the above options at various points in my career, and they are both traumatic and costly.

Before embarking on a "hardball" approach, you had better ensure that you have the support of the board members in writing for your plan of action and an understanding on their part of the financial exposure.

In some instances, there is no option if the company is ever to be made whole, but, again, it is a court of last resort. Be sure that, prior to embarking on any program of this type, you hire the best labor attorney you can find and have him guide you through the intricacies of the labor laws so that you make no costly violations.

COMMUNICATIONS

At the beginning of this chapter I said that it is imperative during a renewal that people be kept informed, but so far I haven't talked about communications and communicating methods.

I described management committee meetings earlier, but what about the people in the plant? How do you communicate with them? I have effectively used several methods that are a modified quality circle approach. You may be familiar with quality circle, as the Japanese approach to small group interaction between employees and management (by the way, I admire and advocate the use of quality circles, whenever possible).

During a renewal, a multitude of changes will be occurring simultaneously, and this upheaval will cause nervousness and apprehension among the troops. The only way to dispel this uneasiness is to do two things:

1. Meet with your people on a regular basis.
2. Espouse management by touching.

Regular Plant Meetings

Meeting with the people implies different things to me than it does to most managers. I do not believe in unidirectional meetings. At the typical plant meeting, a bunch of executives breeze in from headquarters, lecture a bunch of stone-faced factory employees about management's perceptions, and then breeze out of town for another year.

I advocate at least quarterly meetings *on company time*, and during the initial phases of a renewal these meetings should be held monthly. These meetings are held with everybody—workers, clerical personnel, vice presidents, managers—*everybody*, and no excuses should be accepted from managers for nonattendance. On each of the seats are a pencil and a three-by-five-inch card so that employees may ask any question anonymously of the management if they wish.

The rules of this meeting are simple:

1. All parties must communicate with absolute honesty and candor.
2. If a question cannot be answered at the meeting, the answer must be posted within twenty-four hours.
3. No question is too difficult or too simple to be answered.

The format is as follows: The CEO gets up in front of the troops and tells them what is going on. He states that there are going to be some changes in the way the company does business and that people will be informed of the changes. Perhaps the CEO informs them of some steps that are going to be taken, such as holding meetings like this (and the rules under which they will be conducted), establishing an open-door policy, instituting new benefits, and so on. Then he turns the floor over to specific department heads to tell about some of the things they are doing. The meeting should be upbeat and positive in nature.

The floor is then opened for questions written on the cards supplied. Each question is initially fielded by the CEO and then passed to the officer in charge of that area for response.

It is when you get no questions that you have problems, so it is smart to "seed" the first session with some knotty questions that are on everyone's mind just to get the ball rolling. But if all goes according to plan, communication will flow fast and furiously in later meetings. We got to the point in one company at which we felt we could ask each other virtually any question, and management even got a few unsolicited plaudits from the work force in the form of comments from the floor. We also had one employee comment on the personal hygiene of one of his fellow workers at the general meeting and asked how we could get him to bathe more often. So be prepared for anything.

Management by Touching

The second step is management by touching, first in the form of the plant walk-through. I have always made it a habit to walk through our plant facilities once a day when I am in the office and to demand walk-throughs from all my managers. There is no surer way of feeling the "pace" of the production facilities, getting to know the people who build the product, and fielding problems as they occur than the walk-through.

This is illustrated by the horror story of one company where I had taken over as president. I was on a walk-through and stopped to visit with a drill press operator who happened to be a deaf-mute. (I speak in sign language, so I was able to converse with her.) After asking her "how things were" and if there was anything I could do to help her do her job in an easier manner, I asked her to come visit me upstairs in my office sometime. Her answer amazed me. She said that the plant workers had been told not to come "upstairs" because they were "dirty," and she had never been up to the offices. I asked how long she had worked there, and she said, "Twenty-three years." Now this company had a bad union/management situation, and it is fairly obvious why. The office manager had discouraged all contact between "office" people and plant people and helped create an "us/them" situation.

It is *imperative* to break down this wall between

management and operating personnel and keep it down. This means that, if the company has a problem, everyone helps in coming up with suggested courses of action through the internal network.

I have had people on the line tell me that that they are not pleased with their productivity and feel that they could increase output with the addition of a certain piece of equipment. If communication channels are open, this suggestion gets fed back up through the foreman, and then management can take rapid action on the suggestion.

I strongly encourage weekly *work action group meetings* held by foremen to generate product and process improvements, which in turn are converted into written suggestions and transmitted to management for action. This process is called a *quality circle*.

By this time your people are fully on board, they are pulling with you instead of against you, and from a productivity and service standpoint you have geared your operations for an improvement or turnaround. You can now take the ultimate step and move to a profit-sharing mode. That is, share your potential new profits with the people who are helping you achieve them through an incentive plan or share part of the company through an employee stock option plan (ESOP) with your employees. This is an individual management decision, and I will not elaborate on it here.

You may have been wondering why I have not yet talked about marketing and sales. These *are* crucial areas in any renewal or turnaround, but you are not ready to attack these areas until you deal with all the matters we've discussed through this chapter.

6
MARKETING
or *Where Did the Buyers Go?*

MARKET RESEARCH MADE EASY

What are your markets? How big are they? Where should you be concentrating your efforts?

When I first took over one company, its market share was 2 percent of the available market, primarily because it had overlooked its primary buying influence. By merely reorienting our market thrust, we were able to represent 30 percent of the market within three years. Now getting your share of the market is not quite that easy, but the first step is doing your basic research to find your market needs and identify the buying influences.

The airlines have done this step very effectively by

identifying their primary users as businesspeople and then instituting the "frequent flyer" programs to generate some form of "brand" loyalty. The result has been impressive. A recent survey of frequent flyers showed that approximately 60 percent of those who choose the airline on which they fly do so based on "frequent flyer" programs.

So how do you find out about *your* markets?

Identifying Key Markets

First, you must identify the world in which you operate, or your key markets. I would initially suggest that you sit down with your vice president of marketing, compile a customer list, and lay out answers to the question "What businesses are our customers in?"

Answering this questions is not as simple as it sounds. One business I was in was the soft drink dispenser equipment manufacturing business. You might imagine that everyone whom we sold to was involved in the sale of soft drinks. However, upon analysis the major channels of distribution broke down into the following categories:

- Syrup companies—companies such as Pepsi-Cola and Coca-Cola that manufacture the basic product
- Bottlers—companies that bottle the product and in some instances distribute the dispensers
- National accounts—major direct purchasers of equipment, such as fast-food chains, grocery chains, and convenience store chains
- Equipment distributors

National accounts, as you can see from the preceding list, can be divided into several subcategories. This analysis can provide you with one market segment or, as in the case of some general chemical product, literally hundreds.

You should list not only the market segments you now serve but also those you know exist and are not being served by your company. List your current annual sales to each of these segments and leave a blank for the total market potential of each segment. An example of such a list is shown in chart form on the following page.

You have now filled in a preliminary listing of market segments and your distribution of sales in those market segments. Now you need to find out the total market within each of these segments. You do so through some elementary market research, and if you don't have some young MBA on your staff to do this for you, the sources of this kind of information are a combination of the following:

- Industry and trade associations
- Trade magazines and books
- Department of Commerce Library, Washington, D.C.
- Competition interviews (you have already done these)
- Your own files
- Competitor 10Ks (you have already obtained these)

In less than a week of diligent market research, you can come up with a pretty good approximation of your potential market size and the percentage of the total market that each segment represents.

You now can see if your market efforts are being directed to the larger segments of the market, in which the greatest potential exists. For example, in one company we were selling intensely to a market segment whose total size was less than 20 percent of the market,

LISTING OF MARKET SEGMENTS

MARKET SEGMENT	VOLUME ($) ANNUALLY	% OF TOTAL SALES	MARKET SIZE ($) ANNUALLY	% OF MARKET SEGMENT	% SEGMENT IS OF TOTAL MARKET
A) Syrup Companies	9,000,000	50%	50,000,000	18	28
B) Bottlers	6,000,000	33%	100,000,000	6	56
C) National Accounts	2,000,000	11%	20,000,000	10	11
D) Equipment Distributors	1,000,000	6%	10,000,000	10	5
Totals	$18,000,000	100%	$180,000,000	44%	100%

Marketing, or Where Did the Buyers Go?   107

while our competitors were selling not only to our segment but also to the other 80 percent of the market. By merely redirecting our marketing efforts to the key buyers and leaving the costly, more scattered elements of the market to others, we increased our share while lowering marketing costs.

Identifying Market Influences

You have identified key segments of the market, but your job is far from done. You must now identify the key market influences within that market and/or what makes people within that segment buy. For example, in certain segments of the marketplace, price is the most important factor; in others, quality is most important; in others, delivery or technical assistance is the key.

The only way to identify these factors reliably is by interviewing customers or potential customers in each market segment and asking them what factors are most important. Let me give you some examples. I was, at one point in my career, developing marketing plans for certain chemical products. One market segment I was looking at was the marketing of detergents in paints. Detergents are used to provide the flow characteristics in latex paints.

After two or three interviews, I found that a very small amount of detergent affects the flow characteristics of the paint dramatically. Therefore, price was of no consequence in the buying decision. The key factors were technical characteristics of the product and consistency of quality of the product. Therefore, the way to sell this product to their market was to provide a large amount of technical literature and to emphasize the extent of quality control on the product.

In another instance I had a division in which we were

making a very high-quality product, and the demands of the marketplace had shifted to low quality, low price. So we had a chart that looked like this:

MARKET SEGMENT	PURCHASING INFLUENCES
A) Discount Stores	1. Price 2. Availability 3. Quality
B) Major Department Stores	1. Quality 2. Availability 3. Price

Under "Purchasing Influences" you could list price, delivery, quality, technical assistance, warranty, advertising programs, etc., depending on what you find out in your interviews.

Identifying Who You Are or Are Perceived to Be

While you are interviewing your customers for the purposes of developing an idea of the buying influences, you can also ask the customers' perceptions of what your company does:

"Are we perceived as the lowest-priced seller?"
"Are we perceived as having the best quality?"
"Are we perceived as having the best service?"

You get the idea: find out how others see you. This perception is usually different from the one you have of yourself. You may think of yourself as the high-quality, premium leader in the industry, but others may view you as having the price-cutting, medium-quality product.

Marketing, or Where Did the Buyers Go?

This perception in a company also is often vastly different between management and potential customers, and it is this gap that causes many problems. One company I dealt with thought that its "brand name" and image of quality sold its product. A very quick survey of the market showed that the company had virtually zero brand recognition and that its "quality" was perceived as mediocre to poor, even though the company had spent millions on improving quality.

FINDING A NICHE

You now know what your markets are, what the buying influences in the marketplace are, and how you are perceived among those influences. You must now decide what you want to be when you grow up. That is, what markets do you wish to attack and what do you wish your image to be in those markets? This is *not* to say that you are going to use Madison Avenue "hype" to achieve your target! You will be tailoring your entire marketing and production plan to achieve your targeted goal, so this decision is *very important* to the future of the company.

Since we are talking about renewals, I am going to give you several statements that may help you in your choices:

- Larger markets are easier to penetrate than smaller markets.
- Higher-quality, higher-priced markets are generally more profitable than low-priced markets but are usually smaller in volume.
- Higher-priced markets (top-of-the-line) are less recession-sensitive than middle-of-the-road markets.
- Pricing-sensitive markets are easier to penetrate but,

because of the lack of brand loyalty, are harder to keep and are much more dynamic than high-priced markets.
- Markets where there is a proprietary position, through patents or trade secrets you have, and where there is product demand, are always desirable.
- You should capitalize on your marketing and product strengths when you pick your market niche.

Now you are most likely saying, "I don't need some 'smart-ass author' to tell me these simple points," but you'd be amazed at how rapidly people lose sight of these basic truths. Also, your direction can change after a few years if you so wish it. However, such a change in direction should be planned. In fact, I would recommend a review of markets each year at a minimum.

I would also suggest that you have all your staff participate in the process of selecting a market niche for your company, since it will affect all their careers.

STRUCTURING ONCE A NICHE HAS BEEN CHOSEN

It is all very well and good to select a niche, but now you must develop an action plan to achieve your goals. Let me give you some typical niches and the types of action required:

Marketing, or Where Did the Buyers Go?

NICHE	ACTIONS REQUIRED
Low Price, Adequate Quality	Price structure modification (down) Low-cost, low-overhead manufacture Minimal service Often high promotional costs Rapid distribution Strong receivables/collection function
Medium Price, Medium Quality	Some mark of distinctiveness, service, warranty, delivery, etc. High promotional costs
High Quality, High Price	Strong quality control Strong emphasis on superior performance of product High engineering expense Medium-cost manufacture Strong service function
High Tech, High Price	Strong research and development function Strong manufacturing arm Technically trained sales force High legal fees

In each of these profiles, you need to do a preliminary budget and profitability analysis to determine if the strategy chosen will generate adequate profits for the company in the time frame desired. You may decide that you don't have enough time or money to become a technically superior company in your marketplace and may opt merely to slug it out on price until you can get your company into a more desirable position. There is nothing wrong with any path as long as it leads to financial solvency and profitability.

HOW TO MARKET

Up to now I haven't discussed the mechanism for getting products to market. Products, no matter how good, do not sell themselves. Therefore, you need a vehicle to get your product to market. Some of the more conventional ways are as follows:

The Salesperson

This is a person you hire to sell your product exclusively. You pay the salesperson through either salary or performance incentive (commission) or both. The salesperson's loyalties are to your company alone, and you control his or her actions more completely than in any other form of sales. The more technical the selling, the more you need a dedicated salesperson. The disadvantage of a dedicated salesperson is that the individual is on your payroll, and base compensation, benefits, and expenses are all borne by the company. Therefore, the decision to hire a salesperson is an extremely costly one unless the salesperson can start producing immediately.

The Rep (Representative)

This is a commissioned agent who sells your product (along with others) on commission only. The rep covers his or her own expenses and is not truly an employee of the company. There is little cost, other than training, to bringing a rep aboard, and it is a favorite way for small, undercapitalized companies to get a sales force started. However, using a rep eventually ends up being more costly than using salespeople because, as sales rise, reps' commissions rise proportionately, whereas inside salespeople's costs are spread over a larger and larger base. Reps are harder to control because they are independent businesspeople and do not look solely to your company for their income. Also, if your product constitutes a small part of their line, it is hard to keep their attention. Getting reps to write a call report, short of threatening them with physical violence, is something I have never mastered.

The Distributor

The distributor is like the rep except that the distributor stocks your product. The distributor is a combination of a customer and a representative, and you must keep him or her as well trained as the salesperson while treating him or her with the deference due a good customer. A good distributor can provide repair services and training for customers and can stock products in smaller quantities that you can't handle economically.

Good distributors are hard to obtain but are worth their weight in gold once you've got them. They are often hard to get reports out of, but if they are professional enough, they may be the first to alert you to a change in market conditions.

Direct Sales

Some companies use direct mail as a vehicle for sales. The inside order taker assumes part of the function of the salesperson, while the company relies on advertising for the initial contact with the customer. The advantage of direct sales is that cost is reduced because there's no actual sales force, but the cost of the promotion increases dramatically. Direct sales are intended for "mass market" products in which there may be wide appeal. I say this somewhat hesitantly because more and more sophisticated and costly consumer products are being sold via direct mail. Everything from jewelry to furs to computers is now sold via this medium. It is not being applied widely to technical industrial products and does not work well in this area yet, but who knows?

The Executive Sale

This is a selling method that I have utilized very effectively, especially for breaking into a major account. I feel very strongly that executives in a company often form the best untapped sales resource that a company may have. A potential customer is often flattered to receive a sales call from the president of a company (along with the salesperson, rep, or distributor). The sales call tells customers that they are important to your company and that you want their business. I also insist that the executive ask for an order, just like the salesperson, during the call. You would be surprised at how many times we have received orders in this manner.

The use of an executive not only achieves the sales objective but also helps the staff appreciate the problems of the sales force. Now when I say "executive" I don't mean only people in the sales function. I mean the vice president of finance, the vice president of manufacturing, the vice president of personnel, etc. Everybody in a company is a salesperson and you can drive that message home by insisting on the use of executive sales.

The Combo Pizza

I suggest you utilize a combination of the preceding sales methods to reach your markets. Your choice depends on what you think will work. If what you've chosen does not work, change it. You may think it is crazy for me to suggest this approach, but doctors don't hesitate to vary their treatment when their patients don't respond to a given medication. The same is true of any of the methods I have given you in all the chapters of this book.

ADVERTISING AND LITERATURE ON A BUDGET

I presume that you have literature and utilize some form of advertising for your business. The first reaction in hard financial times is to cut back on the number of brochures and ads. *This is a mistake.* The objective is to cut back on cost, not on informational flow. Cutting back on literature is like telling your salespeople to drive to their customers' offices blindfolded.

The following suggestions are some of the methods for cutting back on literature and advertising costs without diminishing their effect greatly:

- Use black-and-white instead of four-color print in advertising materials and brochures.
- Hire an internal artist for design of brochures and ads and use your ad agency only for media placement.
- Use combination brochures. That is, combine similar products in one brochure so as to obtain maximum sales impact from a single document.
- Design sales literature so that it fits into a standard-sized envelope.
- Swap the product for air time or print space. (This is very commonly done.)
- Use offset printing or discount printing services for single-page flyers, etc. when quality is not critical. (Be careful of quality here.)
- Never print prices on brochures, since a change in pricing will make the brochure obsolete. Instead, put pricing on separate sheets.

These are just a few tips. In adverse economic times, it is often advisable to increase your promotional efforts. Your literature should always be professional in appearance and reflect the image you're trying to create for your company.

THE TRADE SHOW, OR HOW TO GRATIFY YOUR EGO

When I started this book, I was going to be very

vitriolic about trade shows being the greatest waste of money devised by man. I have mellowed somewhat and realize that there are some industries in which trade shows are good and even necessary. But after a trade show, I feel like I've just eaten a Chinese meal: I'm hungry two hours later.

First, from a pure cost-effectiveness standpoint, I feel that *no financially troubled company has any business being at a trade show as an exhibitor* unless orders are allowed to be taken at the show and are written at the show as a matter of course.

Let me tell you about trade shows and their costs. Here's the usual breakdown for a three- or four-day show:

Booth Space	$ 20,000
Shipping (Booth and Equipment)	5,000
Cost of Booth (Reusable)	5,000
Rental Items	2,000
Cost of Manning the Booth: 5 people (transport and living expenses)	10,000
Entertainment (not lavish)	2,000
Total	$ 44,000

Now, that total is a lot of money for the quality of contacts you make at one of these shows. The cost of one show can support a salesperson for a year.

Second, many companies show new products at shows; often these new products are nonproprietary. I can think of no better way to expose your stable of new products to the competition. In fact, I would highly recommend that the vice president of engineering and the vice president of sales, as well as the president of a company, attend all major shows as observers, but not as exhibitors. This

Marketing, or Where Did the Buyers Go? 117

allows you to feel the pulse of the market and to obtain new ideas from your competitors.

Again, my caveat does not apply to shows that act as the major site for order entry for your product. In that case, you have to evaluate the benefit/cost ratio and decide if attending is worthwhile.

By the way, if you ask your staff if you should eliminate shows, the opposition will be inordinately loud. The reason is that shows often provide a means for all the good ole boys in the industry to get together and chew the fat or for Charlie to get away from home for four days and run wild at company expense.

Now, if you have decided to go to a show anyhow, here is how to make the show productive:

1. Plan in writing who will set up the booth and make that person responsible for it and all ancillary literature, etc.
2. Ensure that booth positioning is satisfactory.
3. Ensure that you are in the convention hotel.
4. Schedule by name and by hour those who will staff the booth.
5. Combine a sales meeting with show attendance.
6. Schedule meetings with key customers well in advance of the show, especially dinner meetings. Have everyone scheduled to entertain a different key customer each night of the show.
7. If you plan a hospitality suite, send out invitations well in advance and ensure that the suite hours do not conflict with some other major show event.
8. Plan the hospitality suite food and liquor purchases in advance and set them up in advance.
9. Make all restaurant reservations well in advance.
10. Plan who is to break down the exhibit and how the

equipment is to get home. (Some people sell equipment at a discount at the show to avoid costly shipping home.)
11. Buy a case of bourbon or scotch and give bottles of the liquor, in addition to their gratuity, to the laborers who help you get your equipment set up and taken down. (Give it to them after they are finished working.)
12. Set up a system for recording all show contacts and a positive follow-up system for calling an interested party after you are back at the home office.

In summary, I still don't think shows are worth it, even with such thorough planning, but if you insist on exhibiting, do it like a pro!

THE MARKETING PLAN—PUTTING IT ALL IN WRITING

I have talked about elements of a marketing plan, projections, pricing, market segmentation, sales force, advertising, trade shows, etc. You have made charts, graphs, comparisons, and strategy sheets. It is now time to put it all into a written plan to remind everyone of what they want to do and how they plan to do it.

The marketing plan should contain the following elements:

- A sales projection, by product, for at least one year and preferably for three years
- An analysis of your competitors, who they are, their strengths and weaknesses, and their market shares
- An analysis of market segmentations
- An analysis of your current market share and projec-

Marketing, or Where Did the Buyers Go? 119

tions of your future market share, by segment
- A listing of your products
- A written description of your projected market niche
- A listing of action steps necessary to achieve your annual and three-year goals, in the categories of pricing strategy and cost, salespeople's strategy and cost, product design strategy and cost (more on this later), advertising and promotion strategy and cost, and administrative strategy and cost

You will note that I mention cost in each category of your action steps list. This list then becomes your budget for the marketing plan for the forthcoming year(s).

The written plan that incorporates these elements is now your bible for marketing, and your people had better be prepared to follow it because it is now in print for all to see.

7
SELLING
"So You Wanna Buy a Duck"

This chapter is different from the preceding chapter on marketing in that here I am going to cover briefly what I feel are some basic principles for motivating a salesperson and the sales force.

The sales force is your link to the customer, no matter what form that sales force takes—whether it is an in-house sales force, a rep force, or a distributor organization—and it is important that this key element be at its maximum efficiency at all times.

The idea in a renewal situation is to obtain maximum productivity from your sales force—to motivate them to new heights on a continuing basis, year after year.

THE TOP SALESPERSON

First of all, let's talk about the psychology of a really top salesperson. A true salesperson is turned on by the excitement of going after a sale and finally closing it after fighting for it. Monetary results are secondary; the true thrill is the chase and capture. The worst thing for these individuals is to have their best efforts rejected for reasons out of their control, such as poor quality of product, failure of the factory to deliver, mistreatment of the customer by another member of the company, and lack of literature or market support. They can stand being told "no" if they know that their products and services are, in their perception, the best available value to their customers, because they can always redouble their efforts to sell if they know their product is right. It is these individuals whom you must and will want to work with to achieve your goals. Their egos can be bruised badly by a strong negative word from one whom they respect, and you can make their day by complimenting them. They may value a $10 loving cup that says "Salesperson of the Year" more than the $1,000 check that goes with it.

Now, how do you direct such a complex individual?

ORGANIZING THE SALES FORCE

The Top Salesperson: The President

I stated earlier that I felt that everyone in the company is a salesperson. I feel that perhaps the most important salesperson is the president. He must interact with the salespeople to let them know that they are not alone. I used to visit all my salespeople periodically to let them know that management fully supported them and to assist them in cracking key accounts. In addition, I would write all my sales personnel a monthly newsletter, letting them know how each of them was doing and how the company was doing in general. Communications on a two-way basis with these individuals were imperative. Often in a problem company, the president is so immersed in financial and other problems that he forgets to break loose and talk to these people. It is imperative to do so.

Establishing Realistic Goals

A part of motivating salespeople is establishing realistic targets for them to strive for in the marketing of product. The technique for doing this is simple. You just ask them for their input in the sales projections for the forthcoming year. You may end up changing those projections, based on certain knowledge that you may have, but all changes should be discussed with the salespeople. I know many companies in which the annual projections are dictated, "top down" decrees of performance. This means that anyone with half a brain can cop out on performance by claiming that the projections weren't his.

I propose a "bottoms up" projection giving the products and pricing that you expect them to work with. Then, when the salespeople "buy off" on a projection, it is their commitment to perform, and you can base their compensation on that plan.

I have also tried to provide salespeople with an indication of the potential total market in their territories so that they know what could be achieved in those territories. Territories, in turn, should be divided so as to provide equal potential for volume so that sales personnel can be rewarded as compared with that potential.

Compensation: "It's not a sale until you've been paid."

I look down at the hairs falling out of my head and onto my desk as I write this section and realize one bitter lesson I have learned that contributed greatly to my baldness: the concept that sales are really not sales until you've been paid.

No matter what compensation scheme you develop for your sales personnel, *commissions should not be paid until you receive your money from the customer.*

In hard times salespeople will often go after marginal accounts to pump up their volume. As I stated earlier, it is OK to accept this business if you know the risk. Since your salespeople are your soldiers on the firing line, they, too, have to accept part of that risk. That means participating in the loss of income if a customer is a slow-pay or no-pay account. Thus the salespeople are motivated to help you collect these delinquent accounts and, even more important, to help select better accounts initially.

When *do* you pay salespeople? I feel that salespeople should be paid within ten or fifteen days of receipt of funds or earlier, if possible.

Motivational Techniques

I am sure that you can go to the library and get any number of books on how to motivate sales personnel. However, here are a few techniques that have worked for me:

Nonmonetary Awards

It isn't all money, as I stated earlier. Salespeople are motivated by awards that go beyond money alone. I don't mean to imply here that compensation should not be more than adequate for top performers. I always tell my sales personnel that it is my fondest desire to see all of them do exceedingly well because, if they are doing well, the company is doing well.

There is the old joke about the salesman who is struck down by a truck while he is crossing 35th Street in New York's garment district. A good samaritan rushes over to the salesman, removes and rolls up his own jacket, tucks it under the salesman's head, and asks him if he is comfortable. The salesman replies, "Oh, I make a living." Most good salespeople make a living, but they need something to help motivate them and keep their eyes on the goal of ever-increasing sales. I mentioned communications with the salespeople earlier, so I will trust that communication is already a given in these discussions. So what can you do now?

Award salespeople items such as rings or trophies for outstanding performance measured against targeted goals. It is said that one of the great motivators in the Super Bowl for the players is not only the money from the game but also the Super Bowl ring. And look at what a relatively sophisticated group like actors will do for the gratification of receipt of an Oscar. What an award does is recognize an individual's superior performance and tell the world that this person has achieved excellence in his or her field of endeavor. These awards should be structured so that they require some effort to achieve but are attainable by each and every one of your sales personnel. They should also be awarded with the greatest amount of fanfare in front of salespeople's peers.

Here are some examples of typical types of awards:

- Achieving highest sale as a percentage of potential market in the salesperson's territory
- Achieving greatest growth in a territory for the year
- Gaining the greatest number of new customers

You get the idea. The award can be a plaque, a pin, or something of that type and should be accompanied by some token stipend.

Motivating the Spouses

Another method of getting to the salesperson is by motivating the power behind the throne and the individual who has to put up with the greatest amount of grief because the individual is on the road or working late. This individual, of course, is the spouse. There are a series of programs that award both partners in a marriage for the salesperson's performance. (These programs should be utilized for reps or distributors as well.) These incentive programs are usually sent to the salesperson's home with letters addressed to the spouse, indicating the award that can be obtained. There are a number of companies that can put these award programs together, or you can do it yourself. These programs really work and can be a lot of fun to administer. The programs usually take the following forms:

Travel Programs. Make awards for performance that allow top salespeople to travel with their spouses or friends to a special resort spot, either nationally or internationally.

Gift Programs. Under these programs, a gift catalog is sent to the house and awards everything from major appliances to fur coats and jewelry items, depending on points the salesperson accumulates.

Scare Technique

Some companies like to periodically scare their reps or salespeople to get them going. I think this technique generally is ineffective and drives a wedge between the company and the salespeople. In the event of nonperformance, when the salesperson has been adequately warned, you should replace him rather than beat him to death. There is nothing more demeaning or back-breaking to a salesperson than continued harassment by the corporation for poor performance. Termination is best for both parties under these circumstances.

ESTABLISHING YOURSELF IN THE MARKETPLACE

Now suppose that your company is in a turnaround situation. In most instances, the plight of your company is well known within your industry, and your company is about as popular as someone with bubonic plague. Even though you may have adjusted pricing, cleaned up the plant, improved delivery, and improved quality, your image with key customers is redolent with the odor of week-old fish. How do you get out of this dilemma? What do you do to call this marvelous renewal to your customers' attention? Management has a need to let the world know about its "new" company. As soon as you feel that your people can truly offer improved service, etc., start utilizing the techniques below, which I've used with success.

1. Write them. I feel that sending a personal note to the CEOs of your major ex-customers is a good first step. This letter should be very upbeat, reiterating the positive steps you have taken with the company and indicating your desire to have them as customers once more.
2. Visit or phone them. The best thing to do next is to phone and visit them to show your interest in reacquiring them as customers. Again, you should reiterate the kinds of things you have done and ask them to *try you* to see if you are telling them the truth.
3. Have them visit you at your expense. This method is the most expensive but also the most effective. Take them on a tour of your facilities and have key staff personnel make presentations. For example, we were having immense difficulties "breaking" into an account with one potential customer be-

cause of bad experiences many years before. After a letter and several meetings in the customer's offices, I suggested a visit to our improved facilities some seven hundred miles away from the customer's home office. I suggested that a senior vice president and his staff come with us. Since our plant was somewhat difficult to get to, there was some reticence on the vice president's part about losing one-and-a-half days just going on a plant visit. I solved this problem by leasing a small Lear jet and picking them up at a private airport near their company offices. The trip was a roaring success, with the large company accounting for almost 40 percent of our sales volume over the next several years. Of course, you can't do this with everyone, but it is certainly worthwhile for key customers and costs no more than flying each of them out to the plant commercially.

4. Advertise that your company is going through a rebirth. You can do so as part of your normal advertising campaign, and it will merely add credence to what you've accomplished with the three other methods.

Meanwhile, Back at the Competition . . .

Now all that I have told you to do presumes that your competition is going to sit idly by while you begin to take good customers away from them. This, of course, is not true. What will happen is that the competition will use every error, mistake, and blunder that your company has made in the past to attempt to keep you out. Your competition will claim that it has heard that you are going bankrupt, that your equipment is falling apart, or that your company is being acquired by a mystery company from Nigeria, which is undercapitalized. You have two options in this case: ignore the dirt or call the CEO of the competitive company (or have your lawyer do it) and threaten to sue the company. In either case, the effect is the same. The rumors eventually die down as you show more and more of what you can do as a company.

8

THE PRODUCT
or "But, Boss, How Did I Know It Would Cost So Much?"

Up to now I have not addressed product and product design modification or production and plant modification. The reason is that these steps are usually longer-term and tend to be costlier than the steps outlined earlier. Product modification may require initial capital investment before returns are seen. With this caveat in mind, let's proceed.

THE PRODUCT AND ITS RELEVANCE TO THE MARKETPLACE

Many times companies find themselves with products whose time has passed or that, for various reasons, have poor appeal. We all can name products—CB radios, snowmobiles, buggy whips—that fall into this category. These products, as a result of technical obsolescence, lack of market appeal, or market saturation, have had their day.

If you have one of these products, you can expect two effects:

1. Increasing price competition
2. Shrinking market size and increasing market resistance

What these effects translate into is that it will take more and more funds to obtain greater market share. If a line is unprofitable for you, you should begin looking for new products that can utilize the same manufacturing facilities or channels of distribution and phase out the unprofitable line.

Often a company has a product that has great market potential but that costs too much to have wide appeal. In this case, you must decide either to sell to a small market at very high cost or to work on lowering costs and pricing to get wider appeal. *This decision is strictly an economic one.* It is better to sell ten units at $10 profit each than to sell a hundred units at 10¢ profit each. If you devote enough effort to any product, you can reduce costs per unit.

VALUE ANALYSIS

Once you decide to reduce cost and increase volume, you must do a *value analysis* of the product to reduce costs.

There is always the argument that, when you embark on a cost-reduction program, quality will, of necessity, go down. This argument is about as plausible as the fact that frogs give warts. In most instances in which I have attempted to lower product costs, product quality *increases*, and so does product reliability.

In one company that I managed, we were making a product virtually by hand and with little specialized tooling. We were using nonstandard components that were costing a fortune. An upper ceiling was imposed on pricing by the existence of a number of competitors and a few sizable major buyers of the product. The only solution was to reduce costs in order to improve profitability.

We entered into an extensive tooling and standardization program that not only reduced our labor hours per unit from fifteen to five but also improved the performance and reliability of the unit. It also lowered component costs dramatically.

You can use these techniques even if you can command a high price for your product. The consequence is simply that you can garner greater profitability now and have room to move on pricing if the competition becomes greater in the future.

You may ask, "How do I do this?" The answer is the value analysis. Let's first set the context for most product design.

Joe Gump, your product engineer, has been given the parameters of a new widget that you want to design and a time limit of three months to get it developed. In most instances, Joe lays out his design and then buys a whole series of components from a number of suppliers whom he is used to dealing with. In fact, if he needs a special component, such as a pump, he may get his friend over at XYZ Pump Company to design a special pump for his needs, rather than shopping for one that is close to his needs in a standard design.

In three months Joe shows up with a widget, and it works slicker than glass. He then gives the parts list to Harvey, the purchasing agent, who attempts to source some of the components. Not wanting to change the design, Harvey goes back to the same source as Joe for components and ends up buying very special pieces for three times the cost of a standard component. The parts are ordered, the unit is produced, and the cost becomes part of the company line.

Now, if you think the little scenario I just gave you is fiction, examine how some of your own products were developed.

As I said, the solution to this is value analysis, that is, taking each product you make and putting it and all of its components on a table in front of all your staff—representatives from engineering, marketing, manufacturing, purchasing, finance, personnel, and research and development. Ask the following questions:

What is this unit supposed to do?
What parts are extraneous to the purpose of the device?
What parts do we manufacture?
Should we be buying certain parts we manufacture, or vice versa?
What parts are available in standard sizes that we now use in volume that can be substituted for components of the unit? (Screws and fasteners are a favorite item here.)
What major components can be purchased more cheaply in standard sizes from another supplier?
What manufacturing technique can be modified to make the unit easier to produce?
What features would we change to improve the product?

What components can be made of less expensive materials?

What tools would make the unit easier to assemble, and what components should be changed to accommodate that tooling?

What can be done to maximize the quality and reliability of the product without adding cost?

Can the size of the product be changed to make it less costly to ship?

Assign a project manager to coordinate the answers to these questions among all parties. You will need several meetings of this type, per product, until an action direction emerges for redesign.

You will be amazed at the amount of money you can save by employing this technique across your product line, whether it is business forms or complex mechanical devices.

This technique should be used for each old product and certainly for any new product at least every one or two years. You will soon find that many of the parts of your product line are interchangeable and that your raw material inventories will begin to drop.

In fact, I found that people were beginning to think of borrowing components from existing models of products as a base for design of new products. Thus, modularization was occurring, and our service function was becoming easier. Our customers appreciated the ability to get by with fewer spare parts for various models of machines. However, this whole process took more than three years, so don't expect rapid conversions of your entire product line. But we saw savings, beginning immediately.

Thus far I have not broached the issue of research and development. Later in the book, I will discuss this topic in a chapter of its own. Just be aware that a company that has no innovative product skills or, at least, an ability to copy others has a limited life span. You must be prepared to develop, copy, or buy new technology as it comes along if the company is to survive in the long run. There is nothing worse than trying to sell obsolete products.

Lots of companies cut back dramatically on research and development to increase short-term profits. This technique is OK, but remember you are merely deferring that expense, not eliminating it.

QUALITY AND PRODUCT DESIGN

We have discussed quality before, but I have one last comment on this subject. Quality is as much a part of design as it is a part of the actual manufacturing process. By picking quality components, and making the design such that the product is sturdy and the assembly is foolproof, you can solve a good part of the quality issue before the product is ever seen on the factory floor. For example, you can use items such as guides molded into plastic parts to ensure proper assembly. Part numbers marked on components and components that fit each other go a long way toward lowering assembly time and increasing quality.

The Product Life Pitfall

There *is* a pitfall associated with quality, and that is product life. Designers often forget what the objective was in the first place.

Let me give you an example. At one time in my checkered career, I was an engineer designing chemical plants. The company I worked for was a reputable and conscientious oil company that, when it designed a facility, designed it to last for thirty years or longer.

In the chemical business, most products' life span is only five to ten years. Therefore, there was twenty years of overdesign in the company's facilities because it was used to working with oil-refining facilities in which the technology and the product obsolescence were much less than that of the chemical business. The company was, therefore, paying 30 percent more than it needed to for facilities.

Don't do this with products. Do not design a disposable product to last for five years. Match the design to the maximum useful life of the product (with some safety margin).

9
THE PLANT
"The Place Out Back Where All the Noise Comes From"

MANUFACTURING vs. SERVICE INDUSTRIES

If you are about to put down this book because you are in a service industry and I'm about to talk about manufacturing, don't. A lot of what I'm about to say is applicable to any kind of business. Let's look at a comparison of manufacturing and service industries:

- *Physical Plant:* Both manufacturing and service businesses have physical facilities that must be maintained and managed.
- *People:* Both manufacturing and services utilize

people to generate their products or services.
- *Overhead:* Both operations have supervision and overhead items like insurance, supplies, etc.
- *Financial Controls:* Both operations use money and spend it and need control.

Are you convinced? OK, then let's proceed.

THE PHYSICAL PLANT

I can walk into a company or a plant and in five minutes tell you how the company is doing without even looking at the books. I call it "the pulse of the company." You can feel how much hustle there is in the company, and you can see if the company is clean or is dirty and disorganized. If I see trash in the aisles and an "I don't give a damn" look in the eyes of the employees, I know we've got a sick company.

Cleaning Up

The first and most dramatic step I take in a renewal is to clean up the physical facilities. This doesn't mean an expensive investment. It just means soap, water, wax, and a little bit of paint. The objective is to give the workers a work environment that they can be proud of. If it exists already, so much the better.

It is an interesting phenomenon that people who work in sloppy, substandard environments tend to dress in a sloppy, substandard way, and the first signal you get that the company is beginning to operate well is that people throughout the company begin dressing better.

Often I have used both clerical and plant employees who work in the environment to help paint and fix it up. This activity, besides heralding the renewal effort, builds a sense of camaraderie in helping to stand the old company on its feet and energize management.

One area to pay special attention to is the employees' rest rooms and eating facilities. Single these out for special cleanup and painting in bright, light colors to give an upbeat feeling.

Replacing Equipment

I am sure that your plant manager has told you that all your machinery and physical plant are no good and that he can't work with that "blinkety-blank" old junk out there. Be warned. There is a tendency to run wild replacing equipment in a renewal because usually there has been neglect or at least indifference while the company has been going through rough or very good financial times. *Don't do it.* Each investment, no matter what the economic climate, must be planned and executed carefully.

The first thing to do is repair and paint whatever is repairable. It is amazing what a little lubricant or some relatively inexpensive parts can do to fix up operating equipment.

Also, carefully weigh each investment in equipment as to what it will return in savings. Make return on investment (ROI) or payback calculations for each capital investment requested. The idea is to cherry-pick the investments with the greatest return first—remember, this is a renewal. The way to do this is to get your manufacturing people to list the equipment they feel they need and to calculate an ROI based on the savings in manpower or production cost that it will generate. Then rank these investments, listing the items with the shortest payback first. Justify each request on a separate sheet, which should look something like this form:

TURNAROUND
CAPITAL REQUEST

Date _____   Project No. _____

Equipment Description: _____
_____

Cost: New _____   Used _____

Installation: _____

Annual Maintenance: _____

Annual Operation Cost: _____

Why is this equipment needed? _____
_____
_____

Savings Per Year:

Labor _____ People × _____ Rate = _____

Material _____ Units × _____ Cost = _____

                Total Annual Savings: _____

Other Advantages: _____

Years to Pay Back _____   ROI _____

The Plant

The summary should then contain the following information:

PROJECT NO.	EQUIPMENT DESCRIPTION	CAPITAL INVESTMENT	YEARS PAYBACK	ROI
5023	Drill Press (Multiple)	$15,000	.5	200%
5198	Assembly Fixture	3,000	1	100%
5197	Computerized Screw Machine	50,000	2	50%

You now have a basis from which to make a rational business decision or plant investment.

My major problem has not been too many capital requests, but rather getting my production people and plant engineers to come up with ideas for new, innovative equipment and applications that would save us large amounts of money. Sometimes when the manufacturing department has been frozen in time for a long period it is very difficult to get it to think of new methods of doing things.

An example of this occurred at one plant where a major operation consisted of the bending of small stainless steel tubing into coils. This operation had been done by hand for several decades, and there was no machinery in existence to do it. The operation was costing an immense amount of labor, and no two coils were the same. I merely hired someone to design and build the machinery for me, machinery that would perform the same function cheaply and more efficiently.

Often it is helpful to hire an outside consulting firm that specializes in plant equipment and design to develop a "master plan" for modernization of your plant that you can follow as time and finances permit. There are a number of these firms, and the best way to hire one is to get a recommendation for one from other companies in your business. I have also used contacts at a university to suggest companies. Often you can find a small, good independent to assist you, rather than one of the larger, more expensive firms.

Hard Tooling

Another major area of physical change that can provide immediate benefits is hard tooling. Hard tooling takes products from a one-of-a-kind job shop mode and puts you in the production line business. You should tool products only where the volume of output justifies doing so. The same economic justification procedure should be used for tooling that is used for equipment. Again, you should cherry-pick those tools that yield the most rapid return on investment first.

In a service business, the equivalent of tooling is computer software, and the same economic considerations apply.

Improving Physical Layout

In the plant or the office, the last physical area that can be adjusted to increase productivity is the physical layout. Laying out a facility to improve work and to reduce material and paper handling is an art unto itself, and there are specialists in this area. I would suggest that you hire one. Often the people who do your master plan for capital investment can also do a master plan for plant layout and design.

PEOPLE

Little things mean a lot. So far I have discussed how to change equipment to get greater productivity, but the simplest way to get productivity is to get your people to give their all 100 percent of the time. It is an interesting phenomenon that when companies, usually of a marginal nature, are sold to the employees, the companies experience a rapid and dramatic increase in profitability.

If you have improved working conditions, as I suggested earlier, then you are most likely beginning to see improved productivity in the plant. I discussed people in depth in Chapter 5, but I feel that some of the things I mentioned there are important enough to bear repeating.

In the plant environment, or anywhere for that matter, people are your most important asset. The little ways that you treat them have a big impact on how well they treat you as an employer.

I talked earlier about getting out on the shop floor to see the employees and to talk to them one on one. This communication is so important, I can't emphasize it enough. The idea, and it is a sincere one, is to generate the feeling that you are genuinely interested in their welfare.

Policies and Procedures

Whenever I go to a company and the personnel director drags out a huge policy and procedures manual, I feel like I am looking at the carcass of an animal long dead. Perhaps it is my entrepreneurial leaning, but I can't stand long, burdensome policy manuals that cover every contingency from "ants in the auditorium" to "zippers, frozen."

I feel that a massive policy manual detracts from the humanity of a company. Any company that can't reduce its hard and fast rules to a document less than twenty-five pages long does not have managers with brains. If you consider that the Ten Commandments were God's policy manual, a company should be able to live with something only twenty-five times longer.

A short policy manual means that your managers and foremen have to take extra precautions to be fair and just in their treatment of employees because they don't have everything covered in writing. It also means that the personnel manager's job is a lot bigger, and he must ensure that supervisors are trained properly in handling personnel situations.

Compensation and Fairness

I feel very strongly about incentives. I think that if you have a profitable company, you should share that profit on a group basis with your employees. In turn, all employees should pull together to get the company back on its feet during adverse business conditions. This means that everybody tightens his belt when the business gets tough and that everybody does well when things are good.

I suggest that you heavily base both management's and workers' compensation on corporate performance through group incentive programs. Of course, it is important to provide to each and every employee a very detailed explanation of how such a system works.

This approach to compensation works very well in a turnaround because it gives the company enough financial latitude to recover while motivating all employees to help the turnaround occur. Combined with the minimal layoff policy I mentioned earlier in the book, it will help offset the effects of business downturns.

Productivity—The Team Approach

As I mentioned earlier, I strongly feel that in any company productivity and quality can be approached as a team effort.

By forming interactive work teams supported by management and listened to by management, you can make improvements in output and quality very, very rapidly.

The methodology is so simple that it is difficult to understand why it is not used by more American companies. It merely consists of a series of weekly meetings in each work group to discuss (surprise!) how to improve productivity and quality. The supervisor acts as the team leader and carries suggestions to the senior committee that okays their implementation. In the case of major capital investments, the financial justification is completed by the work group with finance assisting with the calculations.

Overall corporate policy and operating procedures can be discussed openly at the monthly or quarterly meeting or can be brought up at the work group meetings. No questions raised should be overlooked or left unanswered. The work group, in most instances, can be assigned to implement its own suggestions.

You now have a company that acts like the human body. It has its own cellular repair mechanism.

Safety

Another sign of poorly run shops is that they are generally unsafe, primarily because they are disorganized and the employees are poorly trained. It is amazing that the better a company becomes from a profit standpoint, the fewer the accidents and injuries. Accidents are extremely costly to a company, and, unfortunately, rating factors run on a three-year cycle, so there is no way to get this cost down easily without having good performance for three years. The alternative is to show good performance for a year and to get your insurance carrier to make a special modification of your rating that reflects the action you have taken.

Companies that have become complacent or are in financial trouble usually have neglected safety equipment and procedures for a long time. Safety measures may appear costly to reinstate, but they are well worth it.

In one company I ran we were paying a $70,000-per-year insurance premium over our actual loss experience because of poor safety performance in the past. This meant that we ended up paying $210,000 total over three years in costs that we shouldn't have. You can use the work committees to suggest safety steps as well. It's also important to use an employee safety committee.

To emphasize the importance of safety, I have always provided employees with at least their first set of personal safety equipment (glasses, shoes, etc.) free. Most companies do this.

OVERHEADS

Who Needs Management?

One of the nice things about the approach I suggested earlier with regard to incentives for productivity and utilizing interactive management is that the numbers of managers per employee can be reduced dramatically.

As I stated before, the pervasive force in any organization is the feeling that the size of an employee's staff reflects the individual's status in the organization. This pattern must be broken to reduce staff. To accomplish this, ask these questions:

Which functions in management can I combine to reduce overhead?
How can I utilize "lead" people as working supervisors on the production line?
What is the optimum number of supervisors I need to maximize communication and safety considerations while minimizing pure overhead functions in the plant?

The Plant 149

As I stated earlier, the concept of zero-based budgeting must be applied to the plant as well as to the other functions within the organization.

Production people are extremely adept at protecting their positions. A somewhat amusing example of this is a company I know of that became so enamored with the production planning function that the number of planners outnumbered the production staff and foremen combined. The company not only was spending a fortune on production planning but also was literally paralyzed by the systems that this multitude of planners put together to justify their existence.

It's just common sense; use your best judgment in reducing overhead. If you have trouble deciding what an appropriate size for a given function should be, contact others who are in similar businesses and ask them how many supervisory personnel they have in a given area. People who normally would not give you the time of day are usually willing to trade information on salary levels and manning levels.

Fixed Costs and How to Reduce Them

In running a plant, I am constantly faced with the problem of overcoming fixed overheads—those that supposedly do not change no matter what level you operate at. These are examples of fixed overheads:

- Cost of facilities (leased or owned)
- Light, heat, and power
- Cost of machinery
- Insurance (building and facilities)
- Cleaning service
- Supervisor
- Supplies (not related to production)

There are others, but you get the idea. The first myth I want to dispel is the concept that these costs are fixed. In a renewal, you *cannot view any cost as fixed*. As shown below, "fixed" costs *can* become variable.

Cost of Facilities

Facilities can be partitioned and sublet to others, which then reduces your lease or turns nonuseful space into income-producing space. Many companies, however, object to partitioning and subleases because they don't like the idea of having other people wander through their plant or because they feel "it won't be there when we need it." There are ways around these problems. First of all, you can always build separate entrances for the partitioned space if you can't partition in such a way that you can utilize existing entry and loading docks. You will also have to put up temporary walls in the partitioned facilities to provide a separate entrance and exit so that the lesser personnel will not use the same entrance as your own. Second, you can sublet on a short-term basis, say for one year, so that you can reclaim the space once your business needs grow. You can always sublet other space for a short period of time. In this way you are at least breaking even on the nonused space, rather than losing money each month.

Cost of Light, Heat, and Power

Earlier I discussed the possibility of reducing electrical bills by lowering the peak power requirement of the facility. A facility is charged for two factors: peak demand—that is, the maximum power drawn at any given point during the day—and usage, the total power consumed over the period measured.

To significantly reduce your power bill, bring your peak power usage down by making sure that all large, electrically driven equipment is not started at the same time. This equipment affects your rate from the power company. In one company, we lowered the power bill by more than $100,000 a year by staggering the use of induction furnaces and ensuring that the start-up of these high current units occurred before 7:00 A.M.

You can install computers on your electrical system which will prevent you from rising above any peak demand level you wish to set, or at least warn you if you will rise above the preset level. In fact, you can have the computer turn everything from machinery to lights on and off.

The key to saving power and heat is not using as much. This sounds obvious, but I have visited plants where there are large, empty, heated and lighted spaces with nobody in them. Disconnect the lighting in areas that are not in use. Cut off the heating in these same areas. Use polymer film to seal off unheated areas from these in use and to seal windows and other heat or air-conditioning loss areas. Use dock seals to prevent heat loss at loading docks.

The utilities will often provide free surveys to assist you in appraising the potential areas of energy conservation. Avail yourself of those services.

Cost of Machinery

You can take any of three approaches to reduce machinery costs. The first is to sell machinery. This means that you are making an irrevocable decision to reduce operational capability that will be more expensive to replace when you expand. A sale/lease-back is a method of generating cash based on both your machinery assets and the lease schedule as compared with your payments. You may be able to reduce cash flow and give yourself some working capital at the same time.

A second and more desirable method of covering machinery costs is to view unutilized machinery as being available for "job shop" work. That is, determine what the machinery can do and then hunt for jobs that you can take in house for others that will cover the costs, including amortization and operating costs of the machinery. I have done this quite often in underutilized facilities and have even prepared brochures describing our plant's manufacturing capabilities in order to obtain outside work. This approach also keeps personnel working that you might otherwise be forced to lay off and helps to cover supervisory overheads.

A third method of spreading overheads is through forward or backward integration. What this means is that you partially become your own customer or your own distributor.

Three effects occur when you do this:

1. You gain more control of your sources of supply.
2. You put more work into your factory that can be done by the same personnel you now have, thus spreading overheads.
3. You get the additional profit that you normally would have passed either to your supplier or to your purchaser.

In one company that I ran, we were essentially assemblers of the final product. In this process we used an inordinate amount of stainless steel fittings. When there was a downturn in the economy, I was faced with laying off a lot of workers or finding some productive use for their talents. I decided to make my own fittings as one of many steps that I took. It not only reduced my cost per fitting but also gave me internal control of the quality

The Plant

and the delivery of the product while saving two jobs from layoff.

Insurance

Most people view their insurance as a fixed cost. *It is not.* You can shop for your insurance and get special rate adjustments to get your insurance costs down. If your rates are excessively high because of a poor record, you can ask to be assigned to your state's assigned-risk pool, which often has a rate lower than the one you are paying if you have an extremely bad history.

I covered insurance to some extent earlier, so I won't go on. But by doing some clever negotiation, you *can* reduce your insurance costs.

By the way be sure to report any reductions in payroll to your insurance company so that your premiums go down proportionately. (This is usually done automatically, but check on it anyhow.)

Cleaning Service

Instead of hiring one, hire your own people out of the factory. Make the work team responsible for their own areas and give them enough time to do the job.

The same is true for the office. Heavy cleaning can be done by personnel you can hire out of the existing or laid-off work force at a lower cost than an outside cleaning service. In any case, examine the economics and decide which is the least expensive alternative.

Supervision

By using the concept of working lead personnel and job shop filling operations, you can greatly reduce the cost burden of supervision. Your analysis of the supervisor's job function will complete the maximization of supervision utilization. Again, there is little to be garnered by rehashing that information covered earlier. Just remember that it takes about $300,000 in sales, on the average, to cover the cost of one supervisor's salary and benefits.

Supplies

How many times have you spotted the following situations in an office? Each secretary has her own little cache of supplies and goodies. The photocopy machine is being used for personal items. And the mailing system is being used for personal letters. I am not suggesting that all employees misuse these items; in fact, those who do often are not even aware that they are literally stealing from the company.

Controls to place on these overhead expenditures include the following:

- Department keys and counters for copy machines
- Central supply control with departmental charging for supplies
- Automatic accounting for all telephone calls, including recording the number called and the phone called from, and limited access to long-distance lines (depending on the job)
- Issuance of free safety equipment with return of the old and worn safety equipment

Every company has its own little story to tell about supplies, but my favorite is the one regarding white cotton gloves. One of my factories was a machine shop in which we machined, polished, chrome-plated, and repolished some components. Polishers use white cotton gloves to hold the parts in both preplating and postplating polishing operations. A study of our supplies costs indicated we were using $40,000 in white cotton gloves per year at a cost of less than $1 per pair. I figured out that we were either the most meticulous polishing operation in the United States or that we were providing all the white cotton gloves for the town in which the plant was situated and perhaps for the state. I asked for some accountability, and the usage of the gloves dropped dramatically. I still don't know where they were going.

A second example involves controlling photocopy expenses. One company I know installed electronic keys on its photocopy machines and then reported usage by department. The company's number of photocopies went down by an incredible 100,000 per month or 1.2 million copies per year. If we calculate that each copy costs 10¢, then the company saved $120,000 per year.

The final example is on personal long-distance phone calls. For some ungodly reason, employees don't think that WATS calls cost the company anything. We found one location that was costing us $300 per month in personal phone calls. These stopped when a call-tracking device was installed on our lines.

The upshot of this discussion on "fixed" overheads is that overheads can be brought down and controlled as your business contracts and expands. The idea is to get everyone looking at ways of doing it and getting all the personnel to pitch in.

PRODUCTION CONTROL: A HELP OR A CURSE?

The job of production control is to plan production output to meet sales needs while minimizing inventory, to orchestrate the receipt of materials necessary to meet production needs, and to ensure that the work flow through the plant, from a process standpoint, is efficient.

The computer has become a major tool in the complex job of the production control manager. But often in modern companies, when there is a contraction of business or a turnaround, there is no contraction of the production control effort. I gave you the example of the company in which production control people outnumbered the production management. The size of the production control function beyond a certain minimum often reflects an attempt to solve improper system construction or documentation by people overkill.

The same syndrome exists in the accounting function. It goes something like this: If you can't get what you want out of the system, throw people at the problem until you overwhelm it. This is analogous to painting a barn by hiring a thousand men, giving each a gallon of paint, and at the count of three, having each throw his can of paint at the barn. The barn gets painted, but it's messy and damned expensive.

Here are some guidelines for sensible production control:

1. Develop the simplest system you can for production control that is consistent with your product line.
2. Simplify the number of products and components you use. (See the section on value analysis in Chapter 8.)
3. Develop just-in-time (JIT) delivery of raw materials, as discussed earlier.
4. Keep drawing and route sheets current; update them as they change.
5. Establish regular production planning meetings between production and marketing.
6. In times of recession or retrenchment, insist that

production control contract just as the other departments must.

CONTROLS THAT MAKE SENSE

We have discussed many ways to bring production costs down, but what controls can you, as a manager, institute to red-flag problems in "real time" so that the necessary resources can be brought to bear rapidly? I once heard of the production manager of a large facility who had a red light on his desk that was tied to the power supply for the production line. When the line went down, the red light began flashing and stayed on until the production line began moving again. This is a rather dramatic step but very effective, since each minute of nonproductive output in a plant with 200 employees costs the employer $150 in wages and unabsorbed overheads.

What other types of controls can you use? Here are some control reports I've used:

- Number of employees per day
- Output in terms of dollars of finished goods per day per employee
- Actual hours applied to productive output as compared with hours available for productive output
- Amount of approved overtime
- Daily returns and credits
- Percent of complete shipments
- Daily raw materials purchases, by item
- Daily supplies purchases, by item
- Percent of rejects for rework
- Percent of machinery utilization—time used as com-

pared with total time available for use (weekly)
- Dollar levels of inventory in raw materials, work-in-process (WIP), and finished goods (weekly)
- Variances—efficiency, labor, and material (daily, if possible, or weekly)
- All accidents
- Scrap and material disposition reports (MDRs)

These are some operating documents that measure the pulse of the operations and can be rather easy to obtain once the systems are set up to obtain the data.

You should ask only for controls that you plan on using. This sounds silly, but I have seen companies generate tons of paper as reports that no one ever looks at. Once you become comfortable with the control documents you are utilizing, you usually will be able to spot trends that "don't look right" and take action on them.

Of course, you must do all this document examination in addition to the "hands-on" visits with operating personnel and the work group approach I suggested earlier.

FINANCIAL CONTROLS

Now that I have talked about operating controls in the plant, I would like to discuss financial controls that make sense at the plant operating level.

Standard Costs—A Basic Philosophy

Standard costs are usually engineered standards applied to product cost that reflect the level at which you should be able to produce a product. These standards take into account the expected labor, material, and overhead costs.

My personal philosophy is to make standard costs an

attainable but difficult target for the production group to meet. I feel that, without a tight target to shoot at, most production operations have less incentive to be creative in cost analysis and to take action steps necessary to reduce production costs. And every production group likes loose standards so that it can outdo them and look like heroes.

Therefore, I am strongly in favor of using tight standards as a goal. I also feel that standards should be mutually agreed upon by top management and the operating personnel so that everyone "buys into" the program. As in the sales forecast procedure, those at the operating level should have input into setting standards, given that the standards have a logical engineering base. This interplay can start at the work or quality group level, and often, much to my surprise, these groups will suggest better levels of performance than those indicated as the starting point by engineering.

Variances

Variances are a key indicator as to how you are performing against the standards you set and should be obtained in the shortest time frame possible—daily, if you can get them, or weekly at worst.

In one plant we had the previous day's variances by the start of work the next morning so that we could see where we were straying and take corrective action immediately.

Variances break down into these areas.

Labor Efficiency Variances

These are a measure of the labor it takes to produce product A as compared with the labor you determined it would take to produce product A at standard. This kind of variance can be caused by:

- Low productivity on the line because of lack of effort
- Low productivity because of faulty machinery or design of the parts
- Low productivity because of lack of receipt of material "on time"
- Low productivity because of materials quality problems

Each of the preceding conditions can cause a labor efficiency problem, so to optimize output you must find a mechanism to correct these problems as they occur.

Labor Rate Variances

There is a variance that reflects the use of labor at a higher cost than originally projected. These are the possible causes for this kind of variance:

- Improper rates used in the standard
- Excessive rise of overtime or second shift personnel to produce the product
- Use of more qualified people than necessary to produce the product

Material Variances

This means that you are using more material than originally anticipated to produce the product, which could mean that the design does not match the standards calculation or that you have excessive scrap rates and/or quality problems.

Purchase Price Variances

These are also material variances and they reflect your company's paying more than anticipated for components. Such a variance is a clear signal to get your

Purchasing Department on the stick to obtain lower pricing for materials. Purchase price variances should be obtained by item so that action can be taken with specific suppliers.

Overhead Variances

These are the most insidious of all the variances. They can reflect myriad causes:

- Too much supervisory help
- Excessive downtime or setup time on equipment
- Excessive nonproductive time in the plant for meetings, etc.
- Underutilization of facilities because of a downturn in business
- Overly high expenses in the overhead areas

Look for the Causes

In summary, variances act as signals of some problems that must be corrected. A variance is like a fever when you are ill. It is merely a symptom, and you must still look for the cause in order to cure the disease. Again, the best way to find the cause is to carry the problem back to the work level and ask for positive corrective measures or suggestions within an extremely short time frame. A brief meeting each morning throughout the plant can accomplish this.

Tracking Performance in Real Time, or How to Keep the Horse in the Barn

Until now, I have discussed the kinds of reports that you need to manage the various parts of your business. I have mentioned a whole series of reports and what you can do with them, but I wish to wax poetic for a few moments about the timing of these reports.

The whole idea behind these measurement devices is to provide information fast enough for you to do something about any problems that arise. Reports that provide information for your accountants and the tax man are all well and good but are useless to you as an operating tool unless that time factor is present.

Therefore, you should structure operating reports in a manner and time frame that will help you run your business. Consider all other paper extraneous to your goal of business control. This is especially crucial in renewals, when you don't have time to look at meaningless reports.

Never let accounting run your business. *Use* accounting to run your business, just as you use a wrench or a screwdriver.

In addition, communicate with *all* your people and use them as a source of creative solutions to problems through the methodology I have outlined in this chapter.

10
RESEARCH AND DEVELOPMENT
"Why Should You Know What We're Doing?"

A BASIC PHILOSOPHY

I have presumed all this time that you are running an operation in which you wish to optimize cash usage. At times I have felt that research and development (R&D) is like the description of a sailboat as a hole in the ocean into which you throw money. R&D often is a hole in the operating budget into which you throw money.

In the operation of a company, you have three basic decisions as to R&D operating philosophy that, in turn, will greatly affect the amount of funds you devote to this effort. The three philosophies can be stated as follows:

1. The Leading Edge Approach

This is the most costly approach and can be the most financially rewarding. It is the attitude that your company is going to be the innovator in your industry—the technological leader. You, in turn, will be able to "set prices" until your proprietary position in the form of patents runs out or until the competition finds out how to evade your patents or trade secrets or just plain copies your product.

IBM is clearly an example of a world technological leader that has used its innovation to keep in front of the formidable pack in this highly competitive industry.

2. Copy the Idea, But Do It Better

This is a lower-cost option. You don't have the cost of pioneering an entirely new product or concept, but you do have the development costs involved in doing the idea better.

The Japanese electronic industry for many years intentionally took this approach until it could develop the basic R&D necessary to support a leading edge philosophy. Even to this day, the Japanese share the economic risk of certain R&D by entering joint research ventures.

3. Copy It, But Do It More Cheaply Than Anyone Else

Even this approach gives rise to some developmental efforts, but these efforts are directed toward tooling and manufacturing techniques.

CHOOSING YOUR INITIAL APPROACH

The genesis of the quartz watch industry is a microcosm of these three approaches. The first developers of the quartz watches charged tremendous prices for their unique new devices. Then new generations of quartz watches came along that used LCD instead of LED displays while incorporating day and date and stopwatch functions. Now you can buy a quartz timepiece for less than $5 and throw it away when it ceases functioning.

The question, therefore, is what *you* should do and what approach you should take. This is not a simple question to answer and forces you to ask yourself the following additional questions:

How much money do I have to spend?
How much time do I have?
How do my customers perceive my company?
How do I wish my company to be perceived?
What kind of development skills do I have at my disposal?

The Leading Edge Approach

In a well-funded company the first approach may be the tack that you opt to take. However, as a practical matter it is rare in most companies to have sufficient funds or time to enter initially into a pure R&D, leading edge approach. If this is the niche you see for your company, it is wise to begin considering this approach and planning for it as soon as possible.

Let me give you an example of this. I operated a company in an environment where there were many suppliers and only two major purchasers, both of whom were large and powerful. Because the technology in the industry was around twenty years old, and everyone's product performed an identical function, the products all began to look alike. The two buyers used the competitive situation to keep equipment prices depressed.

My approach was to achieve a marketing and pricing advantage by investing in R&D on a clearly targeted innovative approach that would differentiate our product from others. I had a large financial backer that could support a long-term investment if it looked as though the eventual payout would put us ahead in an extremely limited-size market.

Remember that I have already told you to determine how much financial backing you have and your time constraints.

The development-to-production cycle for a new product is often as long as two to three years and can be as long as five years. In addition, it is estimated that only one in ten new products succeeds.

Pretty frightening? Damn right it is. But pharmaceutical companies make this kind of decision every day, and they have to hurdle the barrier of extensive testing and the FDA, in addition to development and production costs. The payoff, of course, is the speed at which you can recover your investment and garner profits if you "hit."

Improving on an Existing Product

An initial approach for a company that has not been innovative for a while is more likely to be that of taking a new concept in the industry and improving on it. This approach requires relatively low expenditure levels for R&D (quality, not quantity, is what counts here), is applicable to any size marketplace, and requires a relatively limited time frame.

What you must do, basically, is to obtain your best competitor's widget and then critique it, just as you did in your value analysis of your own product. Here, however, you must ask, "How can we improve it to make it more salable for us?" Adding features, improving physical appearance or compactness, and using stronger materials are all methods of accomplishing this goal. Although the financial rewards are not as great as in hitting the "big one" in R&D, neither is the risk. The product is already presumably proven in the marketplace, and your job is merely to devise a way of capturing market share.

Making the Product More Cheaply

The third approach—making it for less—is often as expensive as the second approach because it may involve tooling or new machinery. However, this approach is especially adaptable to those situations in which a very low-priced product will open vast new markets.

I am sure that each of us can name ten products that have gone through this type of phase or at least three companies whose approach is to produce cheaply for mass markets. Again, just because you have one R&D philosophy to begin with does not mean you have to live with it forever.

PICKING YOUR PRODUCT— INPUT SOURCES

No matter what your R&D philosophy, a major barrier to moving ahead is the question of what area in which you should concentrate your efforts. Where should the inputs for new products or product modifications come from? How should you initially screen new products prior to starting to invest in their development?

My favorite tool is the product development committee. It is a think tank group that I generally convene at a remote location, such as a lodge or a quiet hotel setting that is conducive to contemplative thought and relaxation.

I usually ask the following type of people (no more than ten) to be part of the committee:

- Two or three of our customers, usually people I respect

- Two or three people from our sales force (rep or internal)
- Our R&D vice president
- Our marketing vice president
- Someone who is not in the industry but whose thinking process I admire
- The president
- Someone from middle management

I change the committee members each year with the exception of the marketing vice president, the R&D vice president, and the president.

At these meetings we brainstorm for two or three days about what products we feel the industry needs and the priority in which they are needed.

During the meeting everyone has an equal voice and an equal vote, and all are asked to think about their "wish lists" starting at least a month before the meeting. The output of the committee is then passed to the sales force and internal management for comment and may be added to or reprioritized, depending on the comments received.

The final test is then running the output past a select list of customers to determine their response and finalizing it.

There are other sources of input, of course. Here are some examples:

- A survey of your total sales force
- A survey of your customers
- A request of internal personnel for new product ideas
- A review of what your competition has, both through their literature and at trade shows

OK, now that you've got some ideas, how can you boil

Research and Development

these down even further to see how economically feasible they are? The approach is an economic one. How much does it cost and what is the expected payback?

The Marketing Department, with the assistance of R&D, engineering, and finance, is now assigned the task of coming up with the projected development proposal, which looks something like the form on pages 170 and 171.

By now you're saying, "Oh, my Lord, if I did that I'd never get anything done." In fact, most decisions to enter into the most costly investment that a company can make are usually predicated on the words "I like it; let's do it" by the CEO. The form above forces marketing, engineering, production, and finance to collaborate and approve an R&D project. Then you can say, "I like it; let's do it!"

The next step is to ensure that the project is manned with the right people and that the project has a timetable with key progress points identified so that you can easily track your R&D goal.

If I have made any single error in my career it has been in not tracking R&D tightly enough. On at least a weekly basis, you need to receive reports on project budgets from the standpoints of both progress and funds spent. If progress is not satisfactory or funds expenditure is too great, you have adequate time to evaluate action alternatives necessary to bring things back in line or to continue if the investment of extra funds or time is considered worthwhile.

I call this the "no-bullshit" follow-through mainly because under normal circumstances I can be snowed by most R&D people.

The project has come in on time and on budget. You now face the "I don't want my baby to go out in the cruel world" syndrome. The R&D Department never wants to give up projects; it wants to nurture them until they are obsolete. There is a point very close to the projected R&D

R&D PROJECT JUSTIFICATION

Project Description: _____
_____
_____

**Development
Resources Required:**

Manpower _____ Man Days, Total R&D Cost _____

Estimated Development Time _____ Weeks

Special Equipment Required _____

PROJECTED SALES & COST OF GOODS

Year

	1	2	3	4	5	6	7
Sales—Units/Dollars							
Manufacturing Cost							
Labor							
Materials							
Overhead							
Subtotal, Manufacturing Cost							
Gross Profit							
Marketing Costs							
Administrative Costs							
R&D Costs							
Net Pretax Profit							

Projected Capital Required _____

Years to Pay Back _____ or ROI _____

completion date in the justification documentation at which you will be forced to take the project away from R&D and turn it over to production and sales. *This always happens* in one form or another, and the baby is born.

While you have been doing all this R&D control, presumably you have had manufacturing figuring out how to make the product and marketing preparing an introduction plan for the product that conforms with the original justification documents. You now implement those plans. Now wasn't that simple?

11
BEYOND THE BASICS
Other Tips for Turnarounds and Renewals

I am now going to tell you about some things that I haven't discussed before that you can utilize in a renewal. They tend to be a little trickier than the steps I have outlined so far.

INTERNATIONAL SOURCES

A way of getting your product or consumable prices down is to utilize components or raw materials that are manufactured outside the United States. Taiwan, Korea, and Japan have become major sources of low-cost components to companies in the United States. Factors such as monetary exchange rates, delivery costs, and import duties all affect the landed costs of these components, but you can buy landed foreign components delivered to your factory, often at prices lower than those of comparable U.S. suppliers.

The quality of these items is often as good as, if not superior to, U.S. quality, and the warranties on such components are as good as their U.S. counterparts.

The products you buy can also be customer-engineered to meet your needs and need not be off-the-shelf items. Here are the steps to follow in finding such items:

1. Contact the trade missions for the countries that you select. If there is no trade mission in the city in which you reside, call the trade officer of the country's embassy in Washington, D.C., or the consulate in New York City to get a list of recommended companies.
2. Contact these companies via telex and briefly describe the products you are seeking and the volume on an annual basis. In turn, ask for their annual statement and financial references, as well as an indication of their ability to make the product. Check their bank references through your bank or a bank with international correspondents.
3. You now have a list of companies that might act as your source of raw materials or components. Once you have the list narrowed down to acceptable suppliers, send them the drawings and specifications and ask them for quotes based on your annual volume requirements. (Ask for the quotes on a delivered basis.)
4. You now have several quotes. Compare these quotes on a delivered-to-your-plant basis with your domestic suppliers and determine if there are adequate savings to justify proceeding. Choose *more than*

one supplier for your needs. A favorite trick is for a foreign company to get you locked in at a low price for the first year and then to raise prices the second year.
5. The next step is the expensive one. If there is adequate justification for buying from a foreign supplier, you *must* visit the supplier in its country to examine its facilities. This precautionary step is *very* important because you want to ensure that the supplier is what it purports to be. Set up your visits via telex in advance.
6. The terms of the purchase usually consist of a letter of credit in the currency of the country or in U.S. dollars. You can negotiate for a sight draft based on acceptance of the product from a quality basis.
7. Insist on an inspection of goods in the manufacturer's plant by an inspection agency of your choosing. This will cost you 1 to 3 percent of the purchase price of the goods but is well worth it for your peace of mind. A number of companies in the United States specialize in this service and can provide inspection services in plant and prior to shipment.
8. Make sure that you use a good freight forwarder and that the goods are insured.

Is all this worth it? The answer is yes! In most instances you can expect savings of 20 to 50 percent in the landed cost of components at your door. I have seen many companies benefit from this tactic. For example, a customer of mine was purchasing tires for small vehicles from Korea for 50 percent of the amount that he was paying for the equivalent product in the United States. A manufacturer I worked with also saved by purchasing high-quality steel delivered from Japan.

The drawback to all this is, of course, that you must

anticipate your needs one to two months in advance and usually are paying for the supplies thirty days in advance as well. You should include the cost of capital for this period in your calculations as well.

Even if you prefer not to turn to international sources, you may experience a beneficial side effect of this activity. You can inform your U.S. suppliers that you have received competitive foreign bids and would like them to react to the quotations you are getting. Often a domestic supplier will match the competitive bid rather than let it go to an offshore company. Then you have the best of both worlds—a U.S. source at lower prices.

SELLING INTERNATIONALLY

There is a second area of possibility in the international market in a renewal. In even the best of companies, the international market provides a unique opportunity for sales.

In one company I ran, the U.S. market for our products had decreased to a 5 to 7 percent annual growth rate. We had cut heavily into our competitor's position, but our sales growth rate was leveling off because of the lower market growth and the ever-increasing resistance from the competition. Upon investigating the market for our product in the Pacific rim (Asia and Australia), I discovered that a new market for our products was emerging.

I immediately went to this area of the world and set up a number of sales arrangements that netted us an increase in sales of $1.5 million annually.

Now before you rush out and buy your tickets for Pago Pago, there are a lot of "watch outs" involved in selling products internationally:

Beyond the Basics

You need to do some market investigation to determine where your product will fit in from an acceptability standpoint. Obviously, you aren't going to find too huge a market for U.S. chopstick manufacturers in China. Also, there may be cultural problems regarding certain products selling abroad.

An example of this problem occurred while I was attempting to market an extremely portable state-of-the-art electric wheelchair in the Orient. I was in Singapore and talking to a potential distributor of medical devices. After I had given him my number one sales pitch on this unique and innovative device, he was candid enough to tell me why I was experiencing such problems establishing distributors. He indicated that in Chinese culture there were strong taboos against having the ill and disabled circulating among the general populace. The desire was to have sick people hidden away and taken care of by their families. The electric wheelchair made these people mobile, which violated a basic taboo, and hence there was no market. The same taboo did not, however, exist in Japan.

You should also do some prior investigation of the areas of greatest potential for the product or products you wish to market. This means that there must be a commonsense rationale for the use of the product in the country. For example, there appears to be a strong demand for bulletproof clothing in certain South American countries. There is a strong demand for vitamins and health foods in the Orient and in Scandinavian countries. A few calls to the U.S. Department of Commerce or to the "country" officers can often serve as a prescreening device.

The more unique your product, the higher the probability of being able to sell it abroad. Unique and high-sales potential products will have the greatest appeal. I think it would be inadvisable to attempt to sell cast-iron anvils to Japan.

A good way to find out what areas might be good to sell to is to check your competition to see what areas they are exporting to or to check Department of Commerce records of exports of your class of products by Standard Industrial Classification code to various areas of the world. Stay away from areas of the world where there is extreme currency instability or political instability. Good areas, as of this writing, are Europe, parts of the Middle East, and most countries in Asia.

You must visit the countries you are considering to ascertain the size and the potential of the market. If you don't want to invest the funds to do this yourself, hire an export trading company to handle your product. This company, in turn, will act as your international department. The company will want you to give it rights to distribute throughout the entire world for a number of years.

You can sign an agreement with an export trading company; but do so only with the following provisions:

- Give the company the rights as long as it sells X amount of product annually, increasing by 20 percent each year. If not, the contract is null and void.
- Limit the areas of the world to a few until you see how the company performs.
- Obtain a monthly report of activities from the company.
- Be prepared to do some redesign of the product to match specific needs of the country, including labeling changes, etc.
- Do business only on a confirmed letter of credit basis

on a U.S. or equally reputable international banker.
- Warrant parts only and only for a limited period of time.

If you decide to deal with countries on your own, expect to handle these issues in your negotiations. You will have to set up distributors in each of the countries in which you wish to do business, and you will have to control those distributors.

I must state now that generally international business will *not* be as profitable as domestic sales. Some companies actually do make more on international than domestic sales, but this is rare. However, you can generally make incremental profit on this business, and if you are patient, you can make profits on international business equivalent to those on U.S. sales.

The Japanese have learned this lesson well. They are willing to take the long view in investing in foreign markets. The Japanese have put products in the United States at virtually no profit for years until they build up a market. Then, once they have captured the market, they build up prices to give themselves greater and greater profits.

If you are profitable and looking for new markets, there is no reason why you can't do this in reverse. If you are not profitable, the international marketplace can provide a rapid method of filling your facilities and covering overhead.

On top of all this, international business is really fun to obtain. You really meet a lot of interesting people, and it can lead to new lifetime friendships. But remember where your basic business comes from and do not spend a disproportionate amount of time in selling to the international arena.

TIPS FOR SERVICE BUSINESSES

Until now I have concentrated mainly on the manufacturing business because most of my experience has been in this area. But I must reiterate that all the principles I have discussed in this book are applicable to service industries as well.

For example, many of the major public accounting firms have expanded internationally to expand their business base. Hotels can seek international business by advertising for clients in countries where there are a lot of international travelers. They may wish to purchase properties in these countries.

In other areas of asset maximization, I have shown you how to take any company through a renewal. The principles apply across the board. The financial controls I have given you apply to any business. The pricing strategies, with a slight modification, can be adapted to a lawyer's office and to a restaurant.

Let's pick any type of business and apply the principles to it as an example. We'll take a fried chicken chain and enumerate some of the items I have described as action steps and how they apply.

Pricing

Are you getting the maximum amount per menu item based on the quality of the food, the ambiance, and your competitor's price structure as well as the type of clientele?

Financial Controls

Do you have control of the key parameters of your business? Do you know where every dollar is going? Are you utilizing labor to the maximum degree you can? Are you serving the maximum number of stations with the minimum number of persons? Are you paying your suppliers too early?

What formal methods are you utilizing to track food purchases? How much waste is there? Is traffic sufficient to support the operations?

Which operations are making money? Which are not? Should you close down the unprofitable facilities? Do you have reports that tell you the answers to these questions?

Facilities Controls

Are you utilizing all your equipment? Are you in the right location?

Product Development and R&D

What new menu items are you experimenting with? Spicy fried chicken or honey deep-fried chicken? What's the next item on the menu, a salad bar? What investment is required? How long to pay back?

As you can see, everything I have told you is applicable to service businesses. By changing a word or two in this book, you can make it applicable to *any* business.

12
TYING IT ALL TOGETHER

At the beginning of this book, I indicated that it was necessary to decide if your effort was to be a long-term one or a short-term "dolling up" of the company for sale. I have given you both short-term problem-solving techniques and long-term approaches.

Presuming that the company is now in good enough shape to last more than a year, the time has come to prepare a plan. A plan is a budget for the forthcoming year and the succeeding three years in rough format. It's much easier than you might think, because by now you have completely prepared all the elements of a three-year plan, except that you have not quantified your growth in sales for three years.

These are the things you have done that are part of a three-year plan:

- An analysis of competitive products and strategy
- A pricing analysis
- A one-year budget
- A marketing plan
- A production plan
- A research and development plan and priority analysis

All you need to do now is to lay out in writing what you feel will happen by product (folding new products and strategies for the next three years into a pro forma profit-and-loss statement).

You now have a complete guide to your future. This does not mean that such a guide cannot change over the years because it most certainly will change. But now at least there is a direction to your efforts that can be passed on to other managers in written form.

Another major reason for preparing a three-year plan is to obtain money. You now have a document which you can show your banker that demonstrates your ability to control your corporate destiny and a strategic plan for doing so. You now can utilize what you have assembled to seek lenders at a lower rate than you currently have for debt. Usually companies that have obtained external funds without a plan find that a plan provides such a higher level of confidence in their ability to manage the business that refinancing at a lower rate is achievable. A plan also allows ownership to seek venture capital if the company is predisposed to such an approach.

In addition, a plan facilitates the potential sale of a business, although you must make disclaimers as to promises of performance, but at least a potential buyer has a plan to work from.

Tying It All Together

Most of all, the plan gives your company something to work from that will maintain the impetus of the renewal.

Now I am sure you are asking how often should you go through the renewal exercise. The answer is *constantly* and *annually*. By now you're probably saying, "This guy is nuts." But remember that it gets easier each time you do it and takes less and less time because some of the controls you have established are now part of the operating structure and you are using them on a daily basis.

This is not an exercise that can be done once and then forgotten. A renewal is a constant and continuing process. There is a strong tendency for people to step back into bad habits, especially when times are good.

So let's summarize what I have told you in earlier chapters:

1. Initially ascertain what your corporate objectives are. Are you in business for the long haul? Do you want to be the leader in the business? What levels of growth are you looking at?
2. Ascertain, as the Renewal Leader, what your corporate limits of authority are and ensure that you know what the decision process is. Then ensure that others in the organization know and understand what you are trying to do.
3. Talk to your internal people, your customers, your salespeople, and your competitors to identify your strengths and weaknesses. Do this in a nonthreatening manner and consult with other members of the management team to institute steps to correct problem areas, to reinforce strengths, and to push to utilize underdeveloped resources.
4. Take the first step—pricing. Determine what your pricing should be based on your product-by-product analysis of your competitor's true prices, your

competitive advantages and disadvantages, and your desired position in the marketplace. Then implement your pricing plan and begin generating incremental profits.

5. Take control of the finances. Grab the checkbook and find out what items are taking cash and why. Ask lots of questions about items that appear out of line and/or that you have any basic curiosity about. Get the operational managers to think about these items. Get them to watch cash as stringently as you do.

6. Use financial analysis as a basic tool to find high-cost areas and to control key areas, such as accounts receivable, accounts payable, people costs, travel and entertainment, material costs, etc. Zero in on the key cost items in your particular business and concentrate on analyzing the methods of reducing those costs. Use your staff to assist in this analysis.

7. Use your people as an asset. People are not problems; they are assets that can be utilized to the utmost efficiency. The key is communicating and getting everyone on your team. Tell people what the corporate goals are. Then allow them to provide feedback to the corporation on a nonthreatening basis. Act on the good suggestions. Use an open-door policy in handling people. Pass your feeling of respect for all the people who work in your organization up and down the line.

8. Do your market research and decide how you want your company to be perceived. Then design your advertising and pricing goals accordingly. Also, design your product and research activities to meet this end in the long term.

9. Motivate your salespeople and your customers to

sell and buy more. Show them that you are interested in them. Involve them in the business before the product gets to market by utilizing their input in product design and marketing techniques. Use nonmonetary motivational methods, such as awards and trips, to keep your sales force and staff keyed up and at peak performance.
10. Get the right product at the right cost. Value-analyze your products to ensure that the products are being made at the lowest cost with the most standard parts possible and at the highest quality consistent with the needs of the market. Do this for all products. Use tooling for high-volume products. Examine the materials of construction for lower-cost alternatives. Be innovative.
11. Operate your plant as a business. Obtain reports that allow you to spot problems in time to do something about them. Make sure that you are optimizing all your resources, people, materials, and machinery. Treat your people as human beings, whether they are union or nonunion employees. Communicate with your work force and motivate them with a share of the company's growth. Filter out inefficient operations and sources of loss and stop them. Use the financial reports to find the key areas of opportunity.
12. Again, communicate, communicate, communicate. Get people to pull with you on this effort. Renewal is impossible without support from everyone.
13. Develop an intelligent R&D plan. Use your customers, your salespeople, and your knowledge of the market to develop new and innovative products for the marketplace. Decide if you are going to be an innovator, a copier, a low-cost producer and

then follow the strategy that you have decided on. Be ready to change your strategy in the event that market conditions change. Before entering a project, ascertain what benefits will be in terms of sales and profits. Then demand strict accountability of project cost and timing. Be prepared to dump a project if it does not line up to expectations or to accelerate one that shows greater promise.

14. Look at international markets, either as a source of lower-priced components or as a potential market. Be extra cautious in dealing as either a buyer or seller in this vast marketplace. Deal primarily in the more secure areas of the world.

15. Remember, the principles that we have described to you are applicable to all types of businesses. Don't be afraid to modify them to reflect the particular characteristics of your business. These actions of renewal work whether you provide a service, are in retail sales effort, or are in manufacturing.

16. Tie it all together by laying out a three-year plan for your company. Extend your planning out three years in each of your company's disciplines as well. Generate pro forma profit-and-loss statements and balance sheets for the three years. Use your plan to help obtain funds at lower rates than you currently have and increase long-term profits in this manner.

As Walt Kelly said through his charming character Pogo, "We have met the enemy and they are us."

Happy renewal!

INDEX

Accounting
  production controls and, 156
  purposes of, 39
Administrative costs, 78
Advertising, 114
Attrition. *See* Reductions in personnel
Auto expenses, 72

Backhauls, 65
Balance sheet, financial analysis and, 48–58

Cash flow, 43–45
  maximization of, 59

Check signing, financial control and, 29
Commissions, sales motivation and, 124
Common carriers, 69
Communications, 85, 187
  plant meetings and, 98
  plant tours and, 100
Company image, marketing and, 108
Compensation, 146
  for sales force, 124
Competitors
  information from, 25, 41–43
  profit-and-loss statement and, 62

pricing policies of, 16
reaction to renewal, 128
Computerization, 12
Computers
　financial data and, 43
　power costs and, 151
　production controls and, 156
Correspondence for marketing, 127
Cost of product, pricing and, 16
Cost/volume curve, pricing and, 18
Credit, for customer, 48
Crisis, defined, 2
Customers
　company image and, 108
　interviews of, 24, 185
　market research and, 107
　product status with, 18
　re-establishing company with, 127

Deadlines, employee attitudes and, 87
Delphi method, 27
Demurrage, 67
Direct sales, 113
Discounts
　price increases and, 20
　pricing and, 17
Distributors, 113

Employees. *See also* Personnel
　attitudes of, 86
　evaluation of, 89
　motivation of, 90, 144–47, 186
　under-achieving, 88

Energy costs, 76
　physical plant and, 150
Entertainment expenses, 73
Equipment
　costs of, 151
　investments in, 141–44
ERISA, reserves and, 54
Executive sale, 113
Expenses
　of competitors, 62
　control of, 37–39
　operating, 70
　personal, 71–73
　short-interval budgeting and, 61
Facilities, cost of, 150
Fat/lean cycle, 2
Financial analysis, 47–73, 186
　balance sheet and, 48–58
　inventory and, 50–53
　profit-and-loss statement and, 58–73
　receivables and, 48
Financial control, 29–45, 186
　cash flow and, 43–45
　check signing and, 29
　competitors' policies and, 41–43
　computers and, 43
　expenses and, 37–39
　inventory and, 31–37
　in physical plant, 158–62
　service industries and, 180
　weekly statements and, 39–41
Financial officers, policy and, 48
Financial statements, 39–41
Finished goods, inventory and, 32

Firing of employees. *See* Reductions in personnel
Fixed costs, 149–55
FOB shipping, 64
Forecasts, inventory and, 50
Foreign markets, 176–79, 188
Foreign sources for materials, 173–76, 188
Freight damage, 69
Freight in and out, 64–67

General and administrative costs, 78

Hard tooling, 144
Heating costs, 150
Hotel expenses, 72

Insurance
  cost of, 153
  plant safety and, 148
Interviews, 21–27
  of competitors, 25, 185
  of customers, 24, 185
  of managers, 21
  of work force, 24
Inventory
  financial analysis and, 50–53
  financial control and, 31–37
  production reports and, 33
  waste and, 34
Investments, leadership and, 14

Job descriptions, employee evaluation and, 90

Labor hours, reporting of, 35
Labor variances, 159

Layoffs. *See* Reductions in personnel
Layout of plant, 144
Leadership, 11, 185
Leading edge research and development, 164–66
Lease payments, 77
Legal reserves, 55
Lighting costs, 150
List prices, real cost and, 16
Long-term objectives, 9

Machinery
  costs of, 151
  investments in, 141–44
Management by touching, 100
Managers
  interviews of, 21
  selection of, 89
  utilization of, 148
Manual of procedures, 145
Manufacturing industry *vs.* service industry, 139
Marginal accounts, 48
Marketing, 103–19
  advertising and, 114–15
  buying decisions and, 107
  identification of markets and, 104
  international, 176–79
  market research and, 103–9, 186
  plan for, 118
  of renewed company, 127–29
  sales personnel and, 111–14
  targets for, 109
  techniques for, 111–19
  trade shows and, 115–18

Material disposition report, 34
Material variances, 160
Materials control, 53
Meetings
  plant, 98
  for reviews, 81
  work action, 101
Motivational sales techniques, 121-26

National accounts, marketing and, 104

Objectives, establishment of, 9-11, 185
Open-door personnel policy, 85
Operating expenses, 70
Operating supplies, cost of, 77, 154
Overhead
  absorption of, 40
  cost of, 148-55
  fixed, 149
  variances in, 161
Overtime, 35

Patents, 19
Payables, cash flow and, 44
Pension funds, reserves for, 54
Personal expenses, 71-73
Personnel, 83-101, 186. *See also* Employees
  classification of, 93
  communication with, 85, 98-101
  company values and, 87
  evaluation of, 89
  financial, 48
  leadership and, 12
  motivation of, 90, 144-47
  production, 144-48
  reductions in, 91-98
  unions and, 95-98
Physical plant, 140-62, 187
  cleaning of, 140
  cost of, 153
  energy costs and, 150
  equipment in, 141-44, 151
  financial controls in, 158-62
  insurance for, 153
  layout of, 144
  overhead costs in, 148-55
  personnel in, 144-48
  production controls in, 155-58
  safety in, 147
Planning, long-term, 183
Plant meetings, 98
Plant. *See* Physical plant
Policies, leadership and, 14
Policy manual, 145
Power costs, 150
President, sales motivation and, 122
Price increases, 20
Pricing, 15-21, 185
  increases in, 20
  product cost and, 16
  proprietary products and, 19
  quality analysis and, 17
  service industries and, 180
  volume and, 18
Product
  analysis of, 131-37
  complaints about, receivables and, 49
  cost of, 132

pricing and, 16
quality and, 133
design of, 136
improvements on, 166
obsolete, 131
quality of, 136
status of with customer, 18
value of, 132-36
Product development
    committee, 167
Production controls, 155-58
Production personnel,
    144-48
Production reports
controls and, 157
inventory and, 33
Productivity meetings, 147
Profit-and-loss statement,
    58-73
analysis of, 75-82
cash flow maximization
    and, 58-60
shipping costs and, 64-70
Proprietary products,
    pricing and, 19
Purchase price variances,
    160
Purchasing, forecasts and,
    51

Quality analysis, pricing
    and, 17
Quality circle, 101

Rail, shipping by, 66
Raw materials
foreign sources for, 173-76
inventory and, 32
Receivables, 48-50
Reductions in personnel,
    91-98

employee classification
    and, 94
unions and, 95-98
Rental payments, 77
Reports
labor hours, 35
material disposition, 34
production, 33, 157
timeliness of, 161
Research and development,
    163-72, 187
in service industries, 181
Reserves, 53-58
legal, 55
pension fund, 54
for unpaid taxes, 54
warranty, 56
Review meetings, 81

Safety, plant, 147
Sale of business, 10
Sales
commissions for, 124
direct, 113
by executives, 114
international, 176-79
inventory and, 32, 51
marketing and, 112-14
Sales departments
compensation for, 124
goals for, 123
non-monetary rewards for,
    124-26
personnel in, 112
    motivation of, 121-26,
    186
price increases and, 20
spouses and, 125
Sales representative, 112
Service industry
financial controls in, 180

vs. manufacturing
   industry, 139
research and development
   in, 181
Shipping, 64–70
   by boat, 67
   FOB, 64
   by truck, 64–67
Short-interval budget, 38
   profit-and-loss statement
      and, 60
Short-term objectives, 10
   expense control and, 37
Space rental costs, 78
Standard costs, 158
Strategy
   competitors', 25
   leadership and, 12
Supervision in plant, 153
Suppliers
   cash flow and, 44
   foreign, 173–76
Supplies, operating, 77, 154

Taxes, 79–81
   reserves for, 54
Telephone costs, 76, 155
Theft, 35
Three-year plan, 183
Trade shows, 115–18
Transportation, 64–70
Travel expenses, 71
Trucking costs, 64–67

Unions, personnel
   reductions and, 95–98

Value analysis of product,
   132–36, 187
Variances, financial, 159–61
Volume, pricing and, 18

Warranty reserves, 56
Waste, inventory and, 34
Work action group meetings,
   101
Work force. *See* Personnel
Work-in-progress inventory, 33